The Kurds in Syria

Also available

The Kurds in Iraq
The Past, Present and Future
Kerim Yildiz

The Kurds in Turkey
EU Accession and Human Rights
Kerim Yildiz
Foreword by Noam Chomsky

Kurdish Human Rights Project
2 New Burlington Place
London W1S 2HP
Tel: +44 20 7287 2772
Fax: +44 20 7734 4927
Email: khrp@khrp.org

The Kurdish Human Rights Project (KHRP) is an independent, non-political, non-governmental human rights organisation founded and based in London, England. KHRP is a registered charity and is committed to the promotion and protection of the human rights of all persons living in the Kurdish regions, irrespective of race, religion, sex, political persuasion or other belief or opinion. Its supporters include both Kurdish and non-Kurdish people.

The Kurds in Syria

The Forgotten People

Kerim Yildiz

Pluto Press

LONDON • ANN ARBOR, MI

in association with

KURDISH HUMAN RIGHTS PROJECT

First published 2005 by Pluto Press
345 Archway Road, London N6 5AA
and 839 Greene Street, Ann Arbor, MI 48106

www.plutobooks.com

British Library Cataloguing in Publication Data
A catalogue record for this book is available from the British Library

ISBN   0 7453 2499 1 hardback

Library of Congress Cataloging in Publication Data applied for

10 9 8 7 6 5 4 3 2 1

Designed and produced for Pluto Press by
Chase Publishing Services Ltd, Fortescue, Sidmouth, EX10 9QG, England
Typeset from disk by Stanford DTP Services, Northampton, England
Printed and bound in the European Union by
Antony Rowe Ltd, Chippenham and Eastbourne, England

Contents

Map of the area inhabited by Kurds

Introduction

The Kurdish question is one determining the rights of a group of more than 30 million people, a group that is predicted to become the third largest national group in the Middle East. Comprising the world's largest stateless nation, the Kurds are a people whose population and lands form a contiguous geographical area divided between Turkey, Iraq, Iran and Syria with smaller numbers in the former Soviet Union.

Kurdish issues are not widely discussed or written about and existing literature has focused mainly on the Kurds of Turkey and Iraq. The plight of the large Kurdish population in these countries is relatively well-known due to the extent of the atrocities committed against them, their resort to armed struggle, and their international involvement in determining the political future of Iraq and Turkey's future status within the European Union. Whilst moderate attention has been given to the position of Kurds resident in Iran, there has been even less consideration for the Kurds in Syria. As must be acknowledged, this situation is somewhat explicable, not least because researchers face many difficulties in trying to obtain information on the subject of Kurds in Syria. Another underlying cause is that in comparison to other countries with Kurdish populations, the Kurdish population in Syria is relatively small, making the issues faced by their population ostensibly less vital to studies of Kurdish issues.

However, within Syria the Kurds compose almost 10 per cent of the population, a not-inconsiderable section of Syrian society with its own distinct language, culture and ethnic identity. Despite the size of this group, the Syrian state has not accorded the Kurds recognition as a native national or ethnic minority but instead perceives the Kurds as a threat to Syrian national security and unity. As a consequence, the Kurdish minority in Syria has been persecuted, suppressed and marginalized to the extent that even expressions of ethnic identity, such as language and cultural traditions, are illegal and given political meaning. In their attempts to control and contain the Kurdish identity and communities, the state's policy towards the Kurds has involved coercive force, socio-economic and political marginalization, and complex forms of co-option and divide-and-rule policies.

This study developed from the lack of available literature that provided both historical context and events together with the present-day problems faced by Kurds in Syria. Incorporating Kurdish–Syrian relations, regional relations and international relations and issues, the book draws upon interviews with Kurds and other individuals both in Syria and in the diaspora. It draws together existing material on the subject and is intended to act as a platform from which further research and discussion can be launched.

The book seeks to highlight human rights issues pertaining to the Kurds of Syria, whilst contextualizing the Kurdish question in Syria and providing some explanation for its development. By placing the Kurdish predicament within its historical and regional context, the Syrian state's treatment of its Kurdish population can be more easily understood and compared to minimum standards demanded by international law.

The book is divided into three parts, the first of which provides an introduction to the Kurds. In the second part, Syrian history and both regional and international relations are analysed, explaining many of the influences on the Kurdish question in Syria. Finally, part three discusses the discrimination suffered by Kurds in Syria both in the past and present. Examples used within the book are intended to illustrate the forms of discrimination that the Kurds encounter in Syria and the nature of the abuses of their human rights, rather than to provide an exhaustive account of the history of the persecution of the Kurds. Although one of the aims of this book is to provide a more detailed and comprehensive account of the Kurdish predicament in Syria, the nature of the Syrian state prevents the full documentation of the extent and depth of this issue. It is hoped that this book will stimulate further research and debate of the issues involved in both the Kurdish issue as it is defined by the Syrian state and as a wider nationally defined question.

Part One
The Kurds

1
The Kurds

Comprising the largest stateless nation in the world, the Kurdish people are divided between the sovereign states of Turkey, Iraq, Iran, Syria and the former Soviet Union. Possessing a distinct language, culture and history, most Kurds retain a strong sense of national identity that extends beyond the borders of the states in which they live, despite attempts to assimilate them into the national identity of individual states.

Given the complex relations between states containing indigenous Kurdish minorities, the Kurdish identity has proved politically problematic. Consequently, the regimes and institutions within those states tasked with defining and describing the Kurds and Kurdistan have frequently been influenced by 'political' considerations.

It is generally agreed that the Kurds are a people of Indo-European origin who are believed to have settled in the area comprising Kurdistan over 4,000 years ago, although the earliest recorded inhabitants of the Kurdistan region are the cave inhabitants of circa 10,000 BC.[1] There exists archaeological evidence of a people who lived between 6000 and 5400 BC in the Kurdish mountain regions, sharing a distinct 'Halaf' culture. The boundaries of the Halaf culture are similar to the area today referred to as Kurdistan.[2]

Today's Kurdish population is believed to be descended from the Hurri, Guti, Kurti, Medes, Mittanni, Hittites, Mard, Carduchi, Gordyene, Adiabene, Zila and Khaldi kingdoms[3] that ruled the areas of Kurdistan at different times. Of these, the most influential appears to be that of the Hurrians, found in the Zagros, Taurus and Pontus mountains from around 4300 BC onwards. By approximately 2500 BC, the small Hurrian-founded states began to evolve into larger political entities, including the polities of Urartu, Mushq/Mushku, Urkish, Subar/Saubar, Baini, Guti/Qutil and Manna.[4] Qutil became a powerful Hurrian principality, and it is often thought that 'Kurd' is a derivation of 'Qutil'.[5] According to Mehrdad Izady, nearly two thirds of Kurdish clan names and roughly half of topographical and urban names are of Hurrian origin; and many tattoos worn by Kurds on their bodies are identical to motifs found on Hurrian figurines.[6]

Victory records of Assyrian King Tiglath-Pileser I, who ruled between 1114 and 1076 BC, record the 'Kurti' or 'Qurtie' as a people located in Mt. Azu/Hazu, conquered by the King during his mountain campaigns. Alternatively, Professor Izady suggests that the name may be derived from the Akkadian 'Kurtei', 'an indeterminate portion or groups of inhabitants of the Zagros and eastern Taurus mountains', dating its usage back some 3,800 years. Whatever its origin, the name 'Kurd' (or 'Kurt') itself is thought to have been firmly established by the third century BC.[7]

THE GEOGRAPHY OF KURDISTAN

Taken literally, Kurdistan means 'land of Kurds'. The name was first given to a province of the Turkish Suljuk created by Prince Sandjar in the mid-twelfth century AD, a province roughly coinciding with Kordistan in modern Iran.[8] Today, although it does not exist as an independent state, the name Kurdistan is used to refer to the geographical area within which Kurds form a majority. The borders of this area are not fixed and territorial claims vary between different organizations, groups and individuals according to political considerations. Even so, Kurdistan is a distinct and recognized area,[9] stretching from the Zagros and Taurus mountain chains which make up its backbone, extending south to the Mesopotamian plains and northwards to the steppes and plateaus of what was Armenian Anatolia.[10] The area was divided between the Persian and Ottoman empires in the sixteenth century after the battle of Chaldiran. Following the demise of the Ottoman Empire in the early 1900s and the post-First World War settlements partitioning Ottoman territory between European imperial powers, Kurdistan was divided yet again between what are now the modern sovereign states of Iran, Turkey, Iraq, Syria, Azerbaijan and Armenia. Kurdish communities can also be found through the Trans-Caucasian and Asian republics, in Georgia, Kazakhstan, Kirguz and Turkmenistan.[11]

The Kurds have traditionally taken to farming and agricultural production. Until the late nineteenth century, stockbreeding was the most important economic activity in the area of Kurdistan, with nomadic Kurds moving flocks of sheep and goats between the lower plains and higher pastures according to the season. With the advent of international borders, many of these nomadic farmers were forced to settle, although many of them continued their involvement in stockbreeding.[12]

Kurdish areas are agriculturally and mineral rich, producing tobacco, cotton and grain, copper, chrome, iron and lignite. The Kurdish regions account for 15 per cent of Turkish, 30 per cent of Iraqi and 35 per cent of Iranian cereal production.[13] Within the Kurdish areas, concentrations of oil can be found where the official territories of Turkey, Iran, Syria and Iraq meet. Control over exploration, extraction and transportation of oil and the revenues accruing from these fields is a major source of tension between Kurds and the governments of these countries. The increasing importance of oil since the Second World War has meant that these states are reluctant to cede any territory to the Kurds; as a result much of the Arabization, Turkification and Islamification of Kurdish areas can be put down to economic considerations.

The area composing Kurdistan is also rich in water resources, placing it increasingly at the centre of regional disputes and conflicts. The construction of dams on the Euphrates and Tigris rivers has had devastating effects on the many thousands of Kurds who have been displaced.[14] These dams have also had serious effects further downstream in neighbouring states including Syria and Iraq; the issue of water flows between these countries has on occasion brought Iraq, Turkey and Syria to the brink of war.[15]

THE KURDISH POPULATION

The absence of reliable figures for the Kurdish population is an area of considerable contention, intertwined with political considerations. Whilst Kurdish nationalist groups may exaggerate figures, governments of states containing minority Kurdish populations benefit from underestimating the number of Kurds, carrying out few official censuses which recognize ethnic identity as a legitimate category of registration. In Turkey, Ankara only recognized the existence of Kurds within the borders of Turkey in 1990, having previously referred to Kurds as 'mountain Turks' and the Kurdish language as a dialect of Turkish. In Syria, the government considers the Kurdish population to be a result of migration from Turkey and not an endogenous ethnic or national group.

Population estimates consequently rely on historical data, dating from the colonial period, the Ottoman *millet*[16] system and the *tanzimat* reforms of Ottoman Turkey.[17] Since then, rapid and uneven demographic change has occurred within the Middle East. In addition, due to the association of socio-economic marginalization and poverty with higher population growth and fertility rates, the Kurdish population is considered to be growing faster than the Turkish population.

An estimate of the present Kurdish population hovers between 24 and 27 million, with 13 million Kurds in Turkey, 4.2 million in Iraq, 5.7 million in Iran, over 1 million in Syria (between 8.5 and 12 per cent of the Syrian population) and smaller populations in Armenia, Azerbaijan and the Kurdish diaspora.

LANGUAGE

According to Merhdad Izady, there are two main branches of the Kurdish language. Firstly, the Kurmanji group, which consists of northern Kurmanji spoken mainly in northern Kurdistan, and Sorani, spoken in the south. Secondly, the Pahlawâni/Pahlawânik group, which also consists of two main dialects, Dimli or Zaza which is spoken in north-west Kurdistan, and Gurâni,[18] spoken in enclaves of southern Kurdistan.[19] These main dialects are then subdivided into scores of more localized dialects.[20]

Despite this complexity, the more dominant group today is Kurmanj, with Kurmanji spoken in north, west and east Kurdistan and Sorani in southern Kurdistan. There are many similarities between the two dialects, such that understanding and communication between these dialects is reasonable.[21]

Between 1932 and 1943, Celadet Alî Bedir-Xan published the journal *Hawar*, in which he developed written Kurmanji using Roman script instead of Arabic/Persian.[22] Bedir-Xan's script was circulated clandestinely within Turkey, contributing to rising literacy levels within Kurdish communities there. Written Sorani, which had been used by poets and writers in southern Kurdistan during the nineteenth century, was further developed by Colonel Tawfiq Wahbi, who altered the script phonetically following the First World War. However, restrictions on the printing and use of the Kurdish language prevented the Kurds from learning their language and standardizing its use.[23]

Similar restrictions continue to obstruct Kurdish linguistic development and grammatic standardization today. The majority of Kurds are not taught to read or write in the Kurdish languages. In Turkey and Syria, the use of Kurdish in public has been restricted both by law and through intimidation. As a result, teaching and studying of the Kurdish languages has become a clandestine affair for much of the Kurdish population in these two countries.

RELIGION

Traditionally, the majority of Kurds followed the ancient Hurrian religion of Yazdanism and even today the influence of this ancient religion can be found in Kurdish popular culture and religious ritual. Around a third of Kurds still follow branches of Yazdanism, though the majority of Kurds today (approximately three fifths) are Muslim. Some Kurdish communities adhere to other religions and sects that draw elements from Zoroastrianism. Zoroastrianism is an ancient religion dating back to around 500 BC, which is believed to have been deeply influenced by indigenous Kurdish religions; Yazdanism was seen as a contender to the ascendancy of early Zoroastrianism. Many significant Kurdish cultural practices, traditions and symbols can be traced to these two religions, including *Newroz* (the Kurdish New Year celebrated on 21 March), the worship of fire, the rising sun and others. Today, many of the religions practised by Kurdish communities throughout Kurdistan draw upon elements of these religions.[24]

Alevi and Ahl-I Haqq (Yarsanism)

The Alevi religion is believed to have developed in the fifteenth century. Alevis can be found mainly in central Anatolia and there is a large overlap between Zaza speakers and adherents to the Alevi religion. This same overlap can be found with Gurâni speakers and the Ahl-I Haqq religion in southern Kurdistan. The two religions and languages are thought to share the same origins (and, therefore, the people) and that the movement of various peoples through the centre of Kurdistan divided them into two distinct groups. Both religions share the veneration of the Imam 'Ali and both are based on Zoroastrian religious ideas.[25] Non Kurdish Alevis and Ahl-I Haqq can also be found in the same areas.

Yezidi

Around 2 per cent of Kurds are Yezidis, a religion described as a synthesis of pagan elements and other religions including Yazdanism and Zoroastrianism, and elements of the Jewish, Christian and Muslim religions.[26] Yezidi Kurds speak Kurmanji and can be found in areas of Syria, Armenia and the Mardin-Midyat area of Turkey. The small population of Yezidis is testament to the treatment endured by followers of this religion. For believing in the god Shytan, Yezidis have been accused of being devil worshippers and on that basis have been subject to discrimination. As a result, many former followers have converted to mainstream religions such as Islam and Christianity to avoid persecution.

Muslim

The majority of the Kurdish population converted to Islam between the twelfth and sixteenth centuries. Until this time Islam is said to have 'touched Kurdistan rather superficially, and primarily on its peripheries'.[27] Today, around three fifths of Kurds are Muslim, although for many it is seen as the religion of their oppressors. The majority of Muslim Kurds adhere to the Shafi'i school, a religious difference which demonstrates the relative resistance of Kurdish communities to Turkish and Arab penetration; the majority of Turks and Arabs of Mesopotamia adhered to the Hanafi school, which was the official religion of the sixteenth-century Ottoman Empire.[28]

Shi'i

Around 15 per cent of the Kurdish population are *Ithna 'Ashari* Shi'i. These Kurds are predominantly Sorani speakers living in Kirmanshah province in Iran, with smaller communities in Kordistan province. The Fayli Kurds, a group of approximately 150,000 Kurds expelled from Iraq to Iran in the 1970s and 1980s are also adherents to this sect.

Sufi

The remainder of Muslim Kurds belong to one of the Sufi brotherhoods, whose traditions and rituals include fire-eating, self-mutilation and trances. These traditions suggest pre-Islamic roots and influences and signals the importance of social origins.

Other religions

The remaining members of the Kurdish community are a mixture of Christians, Jews, Davidians (Kak'ai), Naqshabandi and Gelani Qadiri.

The main Christian communities in Kurdistan are the Armenians and the Assyrians. Although Armenians and Assyrians can be considered ethnically distinct from the Kurds, a number of communities have merged with Kurdish tribes, with records showing that some Kurdish communities have adhered to Christianity from the mid-twelfth century. In addition, Christian missionaries targeted Yazdani and Zoroastrian Kurds in the eighteenth century, causing many Kurds to convert to Christianity.

Jews have been found in Kurdistan for more than 2,000 years,[29] although the majority of Jews emigrated to Israel following the events of the Second World War and an increase in anti-Semitism. There are around 150,000 Kurdish Jews in Jerusalem,[30] many of whom still identify themselves as Kurdish. Kurdish Jews can also be found in Iran.

2
Kurdish History

'Sykes-Picot Agreement: (May 9, 1916), secret convention made during World War I between Great Britain and France, with the assent of imperial Russia, for the dismemberment of the Ottoman Empire.'

Encyclopaedia Britannica

For many Kurds, May 1916 denotes a turning point in Kurdish history. The Sykes-Picot Agreement set the stage for Kurdistan to be divided according to Western interests; interests which would ultimately deny the Kurds the right to self-determination promised to them in subsequent discussions and agreements.

Following the defeat of Turkish forces in 1918, the possibility to redefine national borders became a reality. Some progress had occurred on this prior to the end of the war, as Husayn, sharif of Mecca, entered into correspondence with Sir Henry McMahon, British High Commissioner of Egypt, over the future of Ottoman Arab lands.[1]

In 1917, the Bolsheviks leaked details of the Sykes-Picot Agreement, the result of secret negotiations between Britain and France in May 1916. The Agreement, negotiated by Sir Mark Sykes and François Georges Picot, removed most of Anatolia from Turkish control with Russia, Italy and Greece all receiving territory as a reward for cooperation. Following the Bolshevik withdrawal from the scheme, the Cossack territories and the Caucasus including Armenia, Georgia and Kurdistan were instead assigned to British influence.[2] The Agreement consequently partitioned Kurdish territory between several areas of influence, subordinating the Kurds and the region of Kurdistan to Allied interests in both Syria and Mesopotamia.

Having thus far tried and failed to achieve an end to the war in a way that would enable both sides to participate in building long-term peace, on 8 January 1918 US President Woodrow Wilson articulated the Fourteen Points, a programme that Wilson considered would form the basis of such a lasting peace. Covering such principles as freedom of the sea and a League of Nations, Wilson also affirmed the principle of self-determination in his twelfth point,

XII. The Turkish portions of the present Ottoman Empire should be assured a secure sovereignty, but the other nationalities which are now under Turkish rule should be assured an undoubted security of life and an absolutely unmolested opportunity of an autonomous development, and the Dardanelles should be permanently opened as a free passage to the ships and commerce of all nations under international guarantees.[3]

This vision for the national groups contained within the former Ottoman Empire was rejected by Allied powers, and the Fourteen Points failed to become a pronouncement of Allied Policy.[4]

THE TREATY OF SÈVRES

As British interest in the region shifted to Mosul for its potential to enhance the future economic and political values of Mesopotamia, Britain began to favour a redefinition of the Sykes-Picot Agreement, which had originally provided for French control over Mosul vilayet.[5] Britain and France entered into negotiations over the extent and status of an autonomous Kurdistan.

Around the same time, fearful of Arab and Turkish rule and the division of land between the imperialist powers, Kurdish tribes began to organize themselves politically and negotiate with the various powers. Opinions within the Kurdish communities varied between those who supported the Western powers, those who were pro-Turkey and those who advocated complete independence. Many Kurds preferred not to commit to one particular standpoint among these different strands of thinking.[6]

Meanwhile, the rising power of Mustafa Kemal (Atatürk) in Turkey, his demands for Turkish independence, his irredentist[7] ideology and his negotiations with the Bolsheviks gave rise to new British concerns about the area north of Mosul vilayet and the protection of their interests in Mesopotamia.[8] Mindful of the need for a buffer zone between the Turks and the British area of control, the creation of an Armenian state and a Kurdish state became of increasing strategic interest for the British. In November 1919, they persuaded respective representatives to sign a Kurdish–Armenian declaration of solidarity against the return of Turkish rule.[9] As the US withdrew from the area, their support for an independent Armenian state was lifted and the question of Anatolia was essentially left up to the British and the French.

Signed in 1920, the Treaty of Sèvres was a peace treaty between the allied forces and Turkey, reducing the territory of the Ottoman Sultanate State which had already been weakened by dependence on European powers for trade and finance. In drawing up the Treaty, a territory in present day south-eastern Turkey and northern Iraq was explicitly designated as Kurdish territory. This territory extended north to the border of the then-envisaged newly independent Armenian state and south to the Syrian Jazira.[10] The Treaty provided for all racial and religious minorities within Ottoman territory; Articles 62 to 64 dealt specifically with the Kurds and Kurdistan and the right to independence, which would be granted by the League of Nations following a referendum a year after the signing of the Treaty.[11]

However, the Treaty was at odds with the Turkish state envisaged by the nationalist Young Turks, the ruling Committee for Union and Progress (CUP) and was a compromise of Turkish territory that the leader of the nationalist resistance movement, Atatürk, would never accept. At the same time as the Sèvres negotiations, Turkey was confronted with external attack, primarily from Greece, and internal domestic civil unrest, particularly in the Kurdish and Armenian areas. The Turkish war of independence between 1920 and 1922 shifted the balance of power between the Turkish state and the British in Turkey's favour, establishing Atatürk's Turkey as a powerful threat to British interests both in Turkey and beyond.

THE TREATY OF LAUSANNE

Before the ink had even dried, the Turkish war of independence caused the Treaty of Sèvres to collapse. Gaining control over the southern Greek invasion, Turkish forces were redeployed to the Kurdish and Armenian regions and the Turks established a military presence in Rawanduz (in Northern Iraq). Britain was placed in a position in which antagonizing the Turks would be detrimental to their interests.[12]

By 1923, Atatürk's forces had overcome the old regime. This, combined with Turkish territorial gains and the declaration of the Turkish Republic, created a threat to British interests in Mesopotamia and Mosul vilayet. A policy of supporting Kurdish uprisings against the Kemalists[13] to secure the northern border of Iraq was encouraged by Greece and Kurdish nationalists, and contemplated by the British. However, striking a deal with the Kemalists was ultimately considered a better option than directly supporting Kurdish rebellions that lacked clear leadership and which might have led to unforeseen difficulties.[14] The British were primarily concerned with protecting their interests in Mesopotamia and preventing the Turks from annexing territory in the area of Mosul under British control. It became necessary to renegotiate peace with Turkey, which made clear that independent Kurdish and Armenian states were no longer feasible.[15]

In spite of previous British references to the Kurds as being an 'autonomous race'[16] and despite their protests to British representatives and having been promised Kurdish self-determination within this territory at Sèvres, Kurdish representatives had no official part in the negotiations. Kurdish nationalists petitioned the British party to the Treaty demanding that their right for Kurdish autonomy be respected. However, British strategic interest in an autonomous or independent Kurdistan reduced in parallel with Turkey's gains in its war of independence and Kurdish protests against the Treaty were consequently sidelined in the face of British strategic geo-political interests.

The Treaty of Lausanne was signed on 24 July 1923 following negotiations with Turkey. The Treaty granted Turkey sovereignty over the territory of Kurdistan now within modern Turkey. Although making provision for the 'protection of the life and liberty to all inhabitants of Turkey without distinction of birth, nationality, language, race or religion',[17] the Treaty failed to even mention the Kurds, who comprised around one third of the Turkish population and 48.5 per cent of the total Kurdish population.

The result of this period of intense political manoeuvring was that by 1923, Kurdistan had been divided between five different states: Turkey, Iraq, Iran, Syria and the former Soviet Union.

THE KURDS OF IRAN (EASTERN KURDISTAN)

Within Iran, the Kurds were recognized neither as a non-Persian minority nor as a national group. In 1946, the Mahabad Republic was established; ruled by Ghazi Muhammad, leader of the Kurdistan Democratic Party of Iran (KDP),[18] it sought autonomy for Kurdish areas of Iran together with democracy for Iran. The Republic lasted a year before the Iranian authorities acted by arresting many KDP leaders, including Ghazi Muhammad. These arrests caused the KDP to collapse. The KDP remained under harsh suppression, and struggled to renew its activities until the 1960s.

The 1961 uprising of Iraqi Kurds, led by Mustafa Barzani, attracted the sympathy and support of Kurds in Iran, who sent material aid to the movement. Soon after, the Shah of Iran began to send direct aid to Barzani, attempting to weaken the Iraqi government. However, the Shah's actions were also calculated to make the Kurdish movement become dependent on such aid, both increasing the Shah's influence within the movement and also weakening the developing bond between the Kurds in Iraq and Iran.

As Iranian Kurds returned from assisting in the Iraqi resistance, the Kurds of Iran were encouraged to begin their own movement and in 1967, the KDP launched an armed resistance movement that lasted for 18 months. However, as the leaders of the movement were killed during battles with the Iranian Army, the movement began to collapse and the uprising was crushed. In later years the Kurds of Iran played their part in uprisings against the Shah, and the Iranian Revolution.[19]

In 1979, the Kurds began to exploit the political vacuum created by events including the Iranian Revolution, the fall of the Shah and the establishment of the Islamic Republic. The KDP declared its own legislation and began to press for autonomy of Kurdistan, whilst the Turkoman and Arab communities did likewise in respect of their own communities. In August 1979, the authorities acted against the Kurds by declaring a holy war on them. Within a month, the Kurdish regions were under military control and military confrontation did not cease until December 1979, when the government began negotiating to grant limited autonomy to national minority groups.[20]

The Kurds were later used as pawns between the Iranian and Iraqi states during the Iran–Iraq War of the 1980s. Each state attempted to weaken the opponent's military powers, a tactic which caused Kurdish villages in Iranian Kurdistan to suffer heavy artillery attacks by both sides.

In recent times, the oppressive treatment of the Kurds in Iran has relaxed. The Kurdish language is now permitted to be taught in the Kurdish regions and books covering Kurdish history and traditions are permitted to be published. Despite this new freedom, restrictions remain in place on the publishing of literature which could be interpreted as promoting separatism, literature on Kurdish nationalism and literature criticizing the Iranian authorities; furthermore, the suppression of Kurdish political rights is still in evidence.

THE KURDS OF TURKEY (NORTHERN KURDISTAN)

When establishing the Turkish Republic in 1923, Mustafa Kemal (Atatürk) gave assurances that the Kurds would be guaranteed a degree of autonomy and that their cultural rights would be respected. However, the new government's radical programme of secularization and unification of the otherwise multi-confessional and multi-ethnic peoples that inhabited the modern state of Turkey, involved the homogenization and re-definition of diverse peoples as Turks. As a result, Kurdish rebellions in the south and south-east of Turkey, by Kurds aware of what they had lost through the abrogation of the Treaty of Sèvres, were brutally crushed. They were subjected to a campaign of enforced displacement involving the destruction of villages and the removal of Kurds from these areas and their replacement with Turks from the interior.[21]

The Kurds remained politically subdued until the national reawakening of the 1960s and 1970s, which resulted in the formal but clandestine establishment of the Kurdistan Worker's Party (*Partîya Karkerên Kurdistan* – PKK) on 27 November 1978. However, following the 1980 military coup, suppression of the Kurdish identity intensified to the point that the use of Kurdish language was forbidden. The state targeted the PKK, causing the leadership and many members to leave Turkey for exile in Syria. In 1984, the PKK began an armed guerrilla movement against military targets and the village guards within Turkey; Turkey's response was to create a 'security zone' along the Kurdish border areas similar to those that had already been started in Syria and in Iraq. This involved the destruction of countless Kurdish villages – condemned by the European Court of Human Rights – and the displacement of thousands of Kurds. Purported motives for the village destruction, which continued well into the 1990s, included removing PKK strongholds and logistical bases among the civilian population, clearing areas that would otherwise be difficult to control of their populations, and after 1990, preventing the extension of the Kurdish autonomous zone in northern Iraq into Turkish territory.

After the leader of the PKK, Abdullah Öcalan was expelled from Syria and captured by Turkey in 1999, the PKK declared a ceasefire and was dissolved.

THE KURDS OF IRAQ (SOUTHERN KURDISTAN)

Iraq was granted full independence by the British in 1932 and by 1946 Mullah Mustafa Barzani had established the Kurdistan

Democratic Party (KDP) in Iraq. A Kurdish uprising occurred in 1961, when the Kurds of northern Iraq rebelled against Abd al-Karim Qassim's government. The initial uprising was crushed, but the Kurds continued with their rebellion until 1970, due to ongoing clashes with Iraq's governments. The accession of the Ba'th Party in 1963 saw an Arabization campaign in the Kurdish regions especially around Kirkuk, an area abounding with oil. Many Kurdish communities were destroyed and the Kurdish inhabitants of many hundreds of villages were forcibly evicted. In their place settled Arabs from southern and central Iraq, shifting the demographics of the region in order to increase Arab control over oil facilities. Further inside Iraq, Fayli Kurds living in Baghdad, Bassara and Amara were deported to Iran.[22]

The rebellion was ended by a peace agreement commonly referred to as the March Manifesto on 11 March 1970. This agreement recognized that the Kurdish nation existed in northern Iraq and provided for autonomous rule for the Kurds over three of the Kurdish provinces within northern Iraq. Unsurprisingly, the agreement did not include autonomy for oil-rich Kirkuk. Disputes over this, the provisions of the peace agreement and general disagreement over the boundaries of the autonomous regions led to an inevitable decline in relations between the Kurds and the government and by 1974, Kurdish rebellion had resurfaced. This time, the rebellion was supported by the Shah of Iran, in part due to the border dispute between Iran and Iraq over the Shatt al-'Arab waterways. As a result of the renewed unrest the Iraqi government placed the Kurds under yet more suppression, with further village destruction and harassment of Kurdish regions in Kirkuk and along parts of the border with Turkey. Yet more Fayli Kurds were deported to Iran from the interior of Iraq.

This uprising was suppressed in 1975 with the signing of the Algiers Agreement between Iran and Iraq and Iran's consequent withdrawal of support for the Kurds. When in 1978 Saddam Hussein gained power and led his country against Iran in what became known as the Iran–Iraq War (1980 to 1988), the Iranians restored their support for the Kurds. However, even this support could not prevent the effects of Saddam Hussein's 1988 Anfal campaign against the Kurds. This campaign consisted of the systematic destruction of Kurdish villages and the arrest and killings of the Kurds themselves by the Iraqi government and army.

The Anfal campaign began in the southern Kurdish regions and spread northward so that by mid-1988, the Kurds were trapped between Iraqi forces pushing north and Turkish forces pushing south to prevent the Kurds from entering Turkey. The pattern in most villages was identical: following bombardment, sometimes with chemical weapons, the village's Kurdish inhabitants would flee, only to be caught by Iraqi troops. Kurdish males were generally taken away and never seen again and it is believed that many of them were executed. Once the village was empty, the buildings were destroyed to prevent resettlement. It is estimated that 182,000 Kurds were killed, with 300,000 more Kurds unaccounted for and over 1.5 million Kurds were displaced as a result of the Anfal campaign.[23]

One of the most well-known Kurdish towns to fall victim of the Anfal campaign was Halabja, which was attacked with chemical weapons in March 1988. Over several days, Iraqi forces dropped combinations of mustard gases and nerve gases including sarin, killing 5,000 civilians within hours and maiming 10,000 more. Thousands more victims died of complications or birth defects in the years following the attack. Chemical weapons were also used in around 40 other attacks.[24]

Following the 1990 Gulf War and its resultant sanctions on Iraq, and emboldened by American rhetoric encouraging the Kurds to revolt against Saddam Hussein's regime, the Kurdish and Shi'i groups rose against Saddam in their respective areas of the country. With no international support provided, these rebellions were quickly crushed and around 2 million Kurds fled northwards toward Turkey and Iran in fear of reprisals. The unfolding humanitarian tragedy finally forced international action and a safe haven with no-fly zones was established in northern Iraq. Kurdish autonomy within the safe haven flourished and developed. Following the 2003 Iraq War, the future for the hitherto autonomous region of northern Iraq is again uncertain.[25]

THE KURDS OF SYRIA

The complexity of Syrian history has been both the cause of increased calls for Kurdish autonomy and independence within Syria and the cause of Syrian authorities associating the Kurds with external powers and separatism. The histories of the Syrian state, the Middle East region and of international relations have all influenced the state's perception of itself and of its Kurdish population. The background to the Kurdish predicament in Syria is essential to understanding state policy towards the Kurds and of Kurdish demands and activities in Syria. It is to the development of this history and to Kurdish–Arab relations in Syria that this book now turns in order to identify how the present situation has arisen.

Part Two
Syria

INTRODUCTION

In comparison with the Kurds in other areas of Kurdistan, the number of Kurds in Syria is noticeably smaller, with a population of around 1.5 million. In July 2003, the US Department of State estimated the Syrian population to be 18.2 million with the Kurds forming 9 per cent of the total Syrian population. Both the UK Foreign Office Country Profile and the CIA World Fact book tally with this Syrian population estimate of 18 million, although these sets of statistics combine the Kurds and other minority groups together to estimate their representing 9.7 per cent of the total population. The Human Rights Association of Syria estimates there are 1.5 million Kurds in Syria, representing between 8.5 and 10 per cent of the Syrian population. Therefore it seems safe to state that within Syria, the Kurds are estimated to form between 8.5 and 10 per cent of the total population, or around 1.5 to 2 million people.

However, Syrian officials do not consider the Kurds to be a national or ethnic minority, even though the Syrian Kurds adhere to different cultural practices and festivals, and notwithstanding the difficulties Kurds often face in adhering to such practices. Despite repeated attempts by the Syrian authorities to assimilate the Kurds into the Syrian Arab identity, the Kurdish identity has remained distinct, although the geographical dispersal of Kurds within Syria has hindered their ability to amass a unified Kurdish social, cultural and political force.

Language

Kurmanji is spoken by Kurdish throughout Syria, with only the accent varying between the Kurd-Dagh and Jazira regions, where the language is influenced from Turkey and Iraq respectively. The Latin-based Kurmanji script was developed by Celadet Alî Bedir-Xan during the French Mandate in Syria and was used in his journal, *Hawar*.[1]

Despite permitting Kurdish cultural organization and expression during the French Mandate, when their mandate ended and Syria gained its independence the French did not secure any guarantees for Kurdish minority rights within Syria. As a result, following the French withdrawal, the Kurds were faced with many measures that made the teaching and learning of Kurdish illegal.

Due to the restrictions on using Kurmanji, many Syrian Kurds are bilingual and speak both Kurmanji and Arabic, although Kurmanji remains the dominant language in the Kurdish regions of northern

Syria. In these areas knowledge of Arabic is often lacking, as most Kurds do not begin to learn Arabic until age five. By contrast, in Damascus, many of the non-migrant Kurdish population now grow up as Arabic speakers.[2]

Religion

Within Syria, the majority of Kurds are Sunni Muslims, although it is reported that a large number of Kurds are rejecting Islam and expressing a renewed interest in what are considered to be 'traditional' Kurdish religions and beliefs, such as Zoroastrianism. Because heterodox marriages are not recognized under Syrian law, it is believed that many Kurds who adhere to heterodox religions are officially registered as Muslims for purposes of marriage and state schooling. Therefore, the official number of Kurdish Muslims is likely to be lower than in reality. Although a significant Yazidi Kurdish community of around 10,000 people exists in the Kurd-Dagh region,[3] its population is declining as the Arabization of Kurdish areas has increased the Islamization of their religious beliefs.

Kurdish settlement

Kurdish settlements in Syria can be found in several main areas, including the Kurd-Dagh, Kûbanî, al-Hasakeh and Damascus.

The Kurd-Dagh

This area is found at the foot of the Taurus mountain range. Kurdish settlement in this region is believed to date back hundreds, if not thousands of years.[4] The Kurd-Dagh is one of the most densely-populated areas of Syria, with a majority Kurdish population. There is a relatively small Arab population dating back over the last 40 years. The main town in the region is Afrîn, and is surrounded by agricultural land and villages. The Kurds in this area are predominantly involved in agriculture and related industries, with the main crops consisting of olives, fruits and tobacco. The area also produces meat and dairy products for the Aleppo market.

Kûbanî ('Ayn al-'Arab)

This is the smallest Kurdish area in Syria, and is found to the north-east of Afrîn, bordering Turkey. The area focuses on agriculture, fruit and vegetable production and livestock farming. Kûbanî is an almost entirely Kurdish town, although in the east and west the towns of Tel Abyad and Jarablus are inhabited equally by both Kurds and Arabs, following Arabization. The Turkish border is closed in Kûbanî, but open for trade in Tel Abyad and Jarablus, which has caused most industrial and economic development to occur in those two towns. The economic marginalization of Kûbanî, which remains underdeveloped, is believed to have been a deliberate policy aimed at dividing and disempowering the Kurdish communities in Syria and Turkey.

Al-Hasakeh province in north-eastern Syria

This region is also known as al-Jazira (the Island) because it was bounded by the Euphrates and Tigris rivers, and was traditionally used for seasonal grazing by Kurdish nomads and Arab Bedouin tribes. As international borders were defined, the Kurdish nomads were encouraged to settle and, noticing the benefits of settled agriculture, the Arab Beduoin soon followed suit.

Many Kurds fled to Syria from Turkey to escape oppression by Kemal Atatürk's forces in the 1920s and 1930s, settling primarily in the Jazira region. The Syrian government often uses this fact to argue that all Kurds in Syria are migrants from other states, but many formerly nomadic Kurdish tribes had already settled and developed agriculture in the region by the late nineteenth century.[5] These Kurds then applied their farming expertise to the once arid land and helped to establish the Jazira region as the 'bread basket' of modern Syria.

Damascus

In the eleventh century bands of Kurds fought in both regular and irregular Muslim armies, the most famous of these soldiers being Salah al-Din Ayubi (Saladin). These bands established cantons in and around Damascus which over time became permanent settlements; as these forces were organized along ethnic or kin ties, so settlement of these groups followed ethnic divisions. Distinct Kurdish quarters were established, including the former cantons of Hayy al-Akrad (the Kurdish quarter), and al-Salhiyya districts situated in the north-east of Damascus on the slopes of Jabal Qasiyun. The Kurds in these areas are more assimilated into Arab culture than the Kurds of northern Syria.

Until Syrian independence in 1946, the centralization of power and the breaking of local hierarchies, a number of Kurdish *agha* families dominated this Damascene Kurdish community. The al-Yousef and the Shamdin families were two such families whose power and influence was linked to the Ottoman establishment and the central authority in Istanbul and based upon ethnic and kinship ties. Although today the power of these families has waned, many Kurds in Damascus occupy a more privileged position than that of their kin in the Kurdish north.

In addition, large numbers of Kurds have migrated to Damascus, Aleppo and other Syrian cities from the Kurdish regions, causing an increase in the Kurdish population of these cities. Many of these Kurds are employed in menial labour and live in the Damascene suburbs. One suburb, Zor Ava or 'built by force' has been built entirely by these migrant Kurds, with no legal authority.

3
Syrian History: 1918–2005

Towards the end of the Ottoman Empire, two drifts of opinion began to emerge in the Ottoman territories, which would eventually influence Arab outlook on the Kurds in Syria. Within Syria, the two opinions were distinguishable by a predominantly urban–rural divide, a divide also reflected within the Kurdish community. From the creation of the French Mandate through to independence in 1946, Arabs increasingly embraced Arab nationalism, which conflicted with the public positions of the Kurds in Syria.

Within the provinces, the Kurdish population and provincial leaders predominantly supported the administrative decentralization policy of the French, as this transferred administrative power to the dominant ethnic communities within a province. For example, during the Turkish war of independence, the Milli tribe of the *Jazira* assisted the French in repelling Turkish advances; this came at a time when the French were considering the creation of a Kurdish enclave in the area stretching from Urfa (Riha) in the west to Cizre (Jazira bin 'Umar) in the east.[1]

Within the urban cities, opinion differed. In Damascus for example, the few Kurdish *agha* families controlling the *al-Salhiyya* and *Hayy al-Akrad* areas supported the central authority in Istanbul, keen to maintain the status quo and their consequent power and prosperity. Quietly opposing Syrian independence, the Kurdish *agha* class did not welcome the Arab Revolt of 1916. However, not all Kurds in urban Syria shared this opinion and many supported both Ottoman decentralization and by 1918, Syrian independence.

At this time, there existed no popular Arab or Kurdish nationalist movements or indeed sentiments, as politics remained an area for politicians and intellectuals. For the Kurds therefore, their public and political position was that laid out by the *agha* classes, owing to their influence and access to political circles and decision-making bodies.[2] Given this it is perhaps conceivable that within ruling circles, the notion that the Kurds opposed Syrian independence and supported external, imperial powers had developed.

THE FRENCH MANDATE (1920–46)

Despite attempts to assert its claim to independence, Syria fell victim to the Sykes-Picot-agreed partition of the Arab world into mandates and by July 1920, Syria was under French control.[3] The French sought to extend their power within Syria by preventing the potential upsurge in Arab nationalism and limiting the power of existing social and political groups. Using a divide and rule policy, supporting minority groups and decentralization to achieve these aims, the French originally intended to create a federal Syria based on three states of 'Alawis, Sunni Muslims and Christians.

As ideas began to be implemented, the actual reality consisted of a Christian state being created in the Mount Lebanon area; the boundaries of which were expanded in 1926 to create Lebanon. By the end of 1926, the Christian state around Mt Lebanon had spread to the coast, incorporating Tripoli, Beirut, Sidon and Tyre; to its east lay the valley of Beqaa, containing a predominantly Muslim population; and the remainder of Syria had been divided into five semi-autonomous areas along regional lines. These multiple divisions within Syrian society succeeded in isolating the Arab nationalists who sought to reunite Arabs into one state.[4]

French rule was overpowering on the Syrian population, with all aspects of society falling under French control. For the Kurds, relations with the French varied. Some tribes, particularly Christian and Aghas, supported the French, as the French policy of decentralization provided them with increased local power.[5] Other tribes rejected French rule, supporting Syrian independence movements alongside Arab tribes. French rule's main impact however, was on Kurdish opinion, which was particularly affected by the issues surrounding Mandate rule, independence and decentralization. These issues began to shape Kurdish thoughts regarding their future position and Kurdish national and political awareness began to increase, particularly with regard to ideas connecting people and their lands to legal and political rights and sovereignty.

Despite this increased political and national awareness, and unlike the upsurge of Kurdish nationalism already beginning to appear in Turkey, Iran and Iraq, the Kurds in Syria were divided both between the different regions and between support and opposition to the French, which hindered the development of Kurdish nationalist political activity in Syria. It was not until 1927 that Xwebûn, a Kurdish nationalist movement directed against the Turkish state, was established in Syria. Having assured the French that it would not incite ethnic or national tensions within Syria, Xwebûn initially benefited from tacit French support within Syria. By 1928, in order to appease concerns amongst the Sunni Arab population of Syria, French support had waned and the movement was closed down, with accompanying restrictions on Kurdish cultural activities within Syria. Xwebûn's activities had caused unrest among Arab nationalists within both Turkey and Syria, connecting Kurdish nationalism in both countries by association and increasing the tension between the Arabs and Kurds in Syria. Simultaneously, the movement allowed many Syrian Kurdish intellectuals to gain experience on issues such as Kurdish self-determination and oppression which could later be used in founding a Syrian Kurdish cultural and political movement.

A further development of French rule involved 'Les Troupes Spéciales de Levant', the Levantine Security Forces who were used for security purposes by the French. Drawing heavily from minority groups within Syria, including the Kurds, 'Alawi and Druze communities, the work carried out by Les Troupes in upholding French control affected the views held by the majority Syrian Arab population towards many minority groups; this further exacerbated ethnic and communal tensions within Syria.

In 1936, the French installed a central Syrian Arab nationalist government, whilst continuing to support the administrative autonomy of areas such as Jabal Druze. In this way, the French both provided concessions to the majority Sunni Arab population, whilst influencing and dampening such powers through relations with minority groups, avoiding what the French perceived to be the threat of Arab nationalism. However, by 1937 there were many localized uprisings that occurred in protest at centralization of power and the domination of Damascene urban notables and elites over the government and the economy. For example, the 'Amudê uprising in the Jazira was led by Kurdish and Christian leaders against the domination of Syria's central administration by Sunni Arabs. As a result of these uprisings, the French authorities promised to establish a special regime for the Jazira region; this took the form of French re-establishment of control. The area's autonomy from central government increased and with the support of the French, a number of Kurdish social and cultural organizations and clubs were established.

All of these events contributed to the increased tension between the Syrian Sunni Arab community and the Kurdish community in

Syria. The consequence of partial Kurdish support for decentralization led the Arab majority to associate the Kurds with communal tension, separatism and threats to their control over central power. Meanwhile the Kurds, having been influenced by French support for local administration, became reluctant to cede power and cultural identity to a central Arab administration in Damascus.

INDEPENDENCE AND ARAB NATIONALISM

Following independence in 1946, Syria was initially governed by the Sunni leadership and merchant urban class, similar to during the French Mandate. These groups held a vested interest in maintaining the status quo, under which they held the majority of power and authority and thus a system similar to that of the Mandate continued for several years. The Syrian parliament was dominated by these groups who augmented their power by preserving relations with France.

However, the traditional political elite failed to combat the negative aspects of a colonial past, and a mood of Arab nationalism and anti-imperialism began to spread through rural Syria.[6] Whilst industrialization brought benefit only to a small sector of the country, economic instability, inflation and unemployment had a huge impact within the urban and peasant population.[7] Politics began to fracture along regional lines and both communism and Arab nationalism increased in popularity, with parties such as the Communist Party of Syria and the Ba'th Party providing increased political mobilization for the marginalized minority and social groups. The ideals of democracy and the concept of capitalism were viewed with distrust due to their association with the previous ruling elite and also due to an increase in the popularity of Marxist ideology.

Arab nationalism underwent a great boost in 1948 with the creation of the state of Israel and the ensuing war for Palestine. Influenced by Arab nationalism, Syrian rhetoric and foreign policy began to be dictated by anti-imperialism and the Palestinian question and the legitimacy of the previous political status quo within Syria was shattered. From 1948, Syria witnessed multiple military coups which swung the country from parliamentary rule to rule by decree to direct military rule and then back again.[8] Instead of the traditional parliamentary political system determining the country's leaders, the military assumed responsibility for regime change and members of the military became increasingly politically active.[9] Secular Arab nationalism seemed to offer the best potential to the new Syrian leaders, offering a solution to the religiously diverse population and helping to integrate religious minorities including the 'Alawi, Druze and Christians amongst others. However, as a national minority, the Kurds were an anomaly which the leaders found difficult to integrate into this new identity.

Adib al-Shishakli conducted two coups in 1949 and 1951. In 1953, he implemented a new constitution and declared martial law. His aim was to form a homogeneous Arab-Muslim state and one of the ways he sought to achieve this was by issuing multiple decrees restricting the use of languages other than Arabic. Despite his best efforts, even al-Shishakli admitted in 1953 that the borders of Syria were 'artificial frontiers drawn up by imperialism' which would account for the ethnic and sectarian mix within these boundaries.[10] After his overthrow by a military coup in 1954, parliamentary rule was reinstated along with the constitution of 1950. Despite the new political and media freedom, Arabist sentiment continued to build among the population.

This Arab nationalism spread across the Middle East in the mid-1950s, especially following the fall-out of the Suez War in 1955 and the Iraqi Revaluation in 1958. In 1952, Gamal 'Abd al-Nasser's Free Officers had staged a coup and gained control in Egypt and on 22 February 1958, Syria, led by the then-ruling National Front, and Nasser's Egypt formed the United Arab Republic (UAR). Political parties within Syria were banned and Nasser dominated both countries' economic, social and political spheres. This union served only to increase Arab nationalist sentiment within Syria, placing the Kurds in a situation where both their national and cultural identity was threatened. At the same time, arrests and misinformation against the Kurds helped to form a perception of the Kurds during this period that continued to shape Syrian policy and public opinion for many years to come.

During Nasser's UAR, Egyptian practices and policies were imposed on Syria. Land reform and redistribution programmes that had previously occurred in Egpyt began to occur in Syria. Political parties were banned, forcing opposition parties underground. Nasser launched campaigns against the Kurds and the communists.[11] Anti-Kurdish propaganda depicted the Kurds as traitors and separatists, linking Kurdish nationalism to Zionism and Western imperialism. Kurdish officers were removed from the military. Suppression even extended to Kurdish culture: Kurdish was prohibited and Kurdish publications were seized; and Kurdish music was forbidden and recordings taken by the authorities; owners and distributors of publications and recordings were often arrested.[12]

Members of Kurdish political organizations also faced pressure. Established in 1957, the *Partîya Demokrat a Kurdistan – Sûriye (al-Partî)* expressed the desire for Kurdish representation and the advancement of Kurdish education and culture in order to counter the negative view of Kurds that was developing in the region. However, this development of Kurdish nationalism in Syria contradicted the goal of Arab unity sought by the Arab governments and fuelled suspicion over Kurdish intentions in Syria due to the inclusion of 'Kurdistan' in the party's name. In a 1960 crack-down on the Kurdish political movement, hundreds of members and associates of the *Partîya Demokrat a Kurdistan – Sûriye (al-Partî)* were arrested. Leaders of the party were detained in Damascus's Mezzah prison and tried for membership of an illegal organization and for plotting to sever a part of Syrian territory. Soon after, the party changed its name to *Partîya Demokrat Kurdi – Sûriye (al-Partî)* to avoid allegations that it advocated the establishment of a Kurdish state which included parts of Syrian territory.[13]

Anti-Kurdish sentiment increased during Nasser's rule due to the ongoing anti-Kurdish propaganda and the campaign of arrest and detention against Kurdish political activists. The 1961 uprising in Iraqi Kurdistan calling for autonomy, led by Mustafa Barzani and the Kurdish Democratic Party of Iraq also impacted on the Syrian perception of the Kurds.[14] Fears of a similar uprising in Syria, combined with the belief that Israeli sources had provided support to Mustafa Barzani's movement, fuelled concerns that Kurdish groups within Syria could be influenced by foreign interference and provide information on Syria's domestic affairs to foreign powers. These concerns led to the perception that the Kurds posed a threat to Syria's sovereignty, security and territorial integrity.

On 28 September 1961, the United Arab Republic was ended by Lieutenant-Colonel 'Abd al-Karim Nahalawi in a right-wing coup backed by Jordan, Saudi Arabia and the Syrian business community.[15] The subsequent declaration of Syria as the Syrian Arab Republic struck a blow to Kurdish hopes for national recognition and equality among the various minority groups within Syria. From then, a renewed campaign of misinformation against the Kurds commenced as part of the Arabization programme within Syria to ensure Arabs formed the majority of the Syrian population.

THE 1962 HASAKEH CENSUS

On 23 August 1962, the Syrian government issued Legislative Decree Number 93, ordering an exceptional census to be conducted in al-Hasakeh province of north-eastern Syria in just one day. The need for a census came from concerns by the Syrian authorities about the number of Kurds that had entered Syria from Turkey since the end of the Second World War. Many Kurds had fled or migrated from Turkey and Iraq in the 1920s to escape persecution by the authorities in the two states and had settled in Mandate Syria. Kurds were also believed to have migrated to the Jazira for economic reasons and others were believed by the Syrian authorities to have acquired Syrian identity documents illegally. The census was intended to differentiate between those who had a right to Syrian citizenship, those who had not and those who had acquired it illegally.

The inhabitants of al-Hasakeh province received no prior warning that a census would be conducted, nor were they given any indication of its consequences. Government representatives went from door to door through Kurdish towns and villages, demanding that the inhabitants prove their residency in Syria before 1945 by providing one or all of the following three documents: a Syrian identity card; a 'family card'; and land deeds that showed ownership and residency before 1945.

At the time of the census, the system of land ownership and occupation in the al-Hasakeh region was traditionally based, with Kurdish landowners owning most of the land on which Kurdish farmers lived and worked. Consequently although the farmers had rights to the land they worked on and many could have been assumed to own the land that they worked, they held no land deeds. As the only form of documentation available to them, many farmers used sheep tax receipts to try and prove that they had lived on that land prior to 1945. However, the importance that these documents and receipts would prove to have had never occurred to the Kurdish farmers and many had not retained proof of sheep tax payments dating back more than 17 years.

Aside from the difficulties of actually proving proof of residency in Syria prior to 1945 within one day, many Kurds deliberately avoided participating in the census to avoid conscription into the Syrian army.[16] The Syrian authorities never provided an explanation for the census to those whom it involved, thus the urgency of registration was lost.

As a result of the census, Kurds were placed into one of three categories:

i)   Kurds who could prove their Syrian citizenship;
ii) Kurds who had their Syrian citizenship removed were registered by the Syrian authorities as 'foreign' (*ajnabi*, pl. *ajanib*). Kurds in the Jazira region were generally considered to be migrants and illegal immigrants and through the census, thousands were officially registered as *ajanib*;
iii) Kurds who did not take part in the census were regarded as 'unregistered' (*maktoum*, pl *maktoumeen*) even if they already held Syrian citizenship.

Overnight, between 120,000 and 150,000 Kurds were stripped of Syrian citizenship.[17]

LT MUHAMMAD TALAB HILAL

In November 1963, head of internal security for al-Hasakeh province, Lt Muhammad Talab Hilal, published a confidential report entitled 'Study of the National Social and Political Aspects of the Province of Jazira' (*Dirasat 'an Muhafizat al-Jazira min al-Nawahi al-Qaqmiyya wa-l-Ijtima'iyya wa'l-Siyasiyya*). In the report, Hilal likened the Kurds to a malignant tumour that had developed in the body of the Arab nation and proposed their excision from the region through a twelve-point plan, consisting of:

- The displacement of the Kurds from their lands;
- The denial of education to the Kurds;
- The return of 'wanted' Kurds to Turkey;
- The denial of employment opportunities to Kurds;
- An anti-Kurdish propaganda campaign;
- The replacement of local Kurdish religious clerics with Arab clerics;
- A 'divide and rule' policy within the Kurdish community;
- The Arab settlement of Kurdish areas;
- The establishment of an Arab cordon sanitaire along the border with Turkey;
- The establishment of collective farms for Arab settlers;
- The denial of the right to vote or hold office to anyone lacking Arabic;

- The denial of Syrian citizenship to non-Arabs wishing to live in the area.[18]

Although the government allege that Hilal's report was an independent report that was never endorsed nor adopted as official policy, many of the problems facing Kurds can be found in the twelve points above. The denial of nationality had already begun with the 1962 census in al-Hasakeh province; and in 1973 the government began to create an 'Arab Belt' along the border with Turkey. Later chapters discussing the Kurds' civil, political and cultural rights provide other examples of the twelve points being implemented in practice. Although actions taken by the Syrian government may indeed be independent of Hilal's report, the parallels of state policy towards the Kurds and Hilal's proposals are striking.

THE BA'TH PARTY COUP (1963)

Following secession from the United Arab Republic in 1961, Syria again underwent a series of power struggles between the government and military and also between Ba'thist and Nasserist elements of the military. These struggles culminated in 1963 with the seizure of power by the officer corps representing the Syrian Arab Ba'th Party.

The Syrian Ba'th Party was based on a combination of principles: ideologies that sought socialist reform of the political system; ideologies that sought an end to foreign imperialist powers interfering within Syria; and nationalist principles seeking the unification of Arab states. The Ba'th Party sought to represent rural Syrians, many of whom had joined the army and graduated to the officer corps and had found in the army a chance to escape poverty and marginalization.[19] One of these groups, the 'Alawi minority, saw huge numbers of its youth joining the army and then the Ba'th Party.[20] Over time the Ba'th Party became disproportionately dominated by the 'Alawi.

For the first time in many years, Syrian politics were no longer dominated by the previous Sunni elite urban classes and were instead run by the military and rural lower classes.[21] However, the Sunni urban elite and middle classes did not accept defeat immediately, providing opposition to the Ba'th Party's rise to power. Internal power struggles within the Ba'thist Party also dominated the initial shift in power.[22] Salah Bitar and Michael 'Aflaq, founders and leaders of the Ba'th Party for several years, were displaced by a leftist group of military and civilian Ba'thists in an internal 1966 coup led by Salah

Jadid, Hafiz al-Asad and Muhammad 'Umran.[23] Another struggle between Salah Jadid representing the Regional Command of the Ba'th Party, and Hafiz al-Asad representing the Military Committee of the Party, ended on 16 November 1970 when Hafiz al-Asad took control, removing the powers from the civilian section of the Party in the process.[24] Following al-Asad's coup, the Syrian political system was completely restructured to ensure its political stability and security.

THE ARAB BELT

During the era of the United Arab Republic, Nasser introduced a policy of land redistribution, removing land from the grip of large land-owners and passing it into the hands of the farming peasantry. This policy was an imitation of Nasser's existing Egyptian land reforms, aimed at limiting land ownership and ensuring an equitable division of wealth. Following Syria's secession from the UAR in 1961 the Ba'th Party upheld this policy, although it was not initially applied in the Jazira region which contained many large estates. The Jazira region was also the location of the 1962 Hasakeh census, which had significantly altered the official Kurdish population in the area causing it to no longer form a majority.

Following the breakup of the UAR, political instability caused frequent changes and delays in intended agrarian reform laws. Once the Ba'th Party gained control, agrarian reform became a major government priority and implementation of the reform was accelerated.[25] In 1965, the Ba'th Party expanded the land reform policy into the Arab Belt policy. Under this new policy, a military cordon was to be created along the Syrian–Turkish border and the Syrian–Iraqi border, much of which was contained in the Jazira region of Syria. This cordon was to be approximately 10–15 kilometres deep and 375 kilometres long. This new policy was implemented by Hafiz al-Asad in 1973 upon completion of the Tabqa Dam.

The authorities initially ordered families in Kurdish villages along the Syria–Turkey–Iraq border area to leave their homes and resettle in other interior regions of Syria that did not traditionally contain Kurdish populations. The authorities then began to move Arab families, who themselves had been displaced by the building of the Tabqa Dam and Lake Asad, into the areas vacated by the Kurds, effectively changing the demographic makeup of the Jazira and surrounding regions. Villages containing up to 200 homes were built to house the relocated Arabs in areas traditionally inhabited by

Kurds.[26] Human Rights Watch reports that homes and agricultural provisions were offered at heavily subsidized rates to Arab migrants along with agricultural loans; as a result many Arabs were persuaded to move to the Jazira region. In the words of a Kurdish engineer interviewed by Human Rights Watch,

> The government built them homes for free, gave them weapons, seeds and fertilizer, and created agricultural banks that provided loans. From 1973 to 1975, forty-one villages were created in this strip, beginning ten kilometers west of Ras al-'Ayn. The idea was to separate Turkish and Syrian Kurds, and to force Kurds in the area to move away to the cities. Any Arab could settle in Hasakeh, but no Kurd was permitted to move and settle there.[27]

In contrast to the Kurdish villages that had been denied basic services including electricity, water supplies and adequate roads, the new villages contained all necessary facilities. Once land was given to Arab migrants, it is reported that many Arab owners did not use the land or relied on Kurdish workers to maintain the land.[28]

These demographic changes did not occur without protest. In one of the many villages along the Arab Belt, the Kurdish inhabitants were a mixture of Syrian citizens and *ajanib* Kurds who had their land expropriated in 1973. During a 1986 demonstration, the Kurdish protestors clashed with the new Arab inhabitants of the village and a young Kurdish girl was killed. Several Kurdish protesters were arrested.[29]

The Jazira region in which the land reforms took place is the primary cotton and wheat producing region in Syria. Oil reserves had also been discovered there. The economic value of the region is believed to be a key reason for implementation of the land reforms and creation of the Arab Belt, with the Syrian authorities being concerned about Kurdish domination of such resources. Within northern Iraq, a large Kurdish population existed around oil-rich Kirkuk. A similar policy of moving Arabs into Kurdish areas to alter the ethnic demographics and reduce Kurdish domination of economically important geographic areas was also implemented both by the monarchy in the 1930s and later by the Ba'th Party.[30]

By the end of 1969, 1.374 million hectares of irrigated and non-irrigated agricultural land had been expropriated. According to official statistics, the following amounts of land were expropriated in each of Syria's provinces: 462,200 hectares in al-Hasakeh; 289,900 hectares in Aleppo; 164,000 hectares in al Raqqa; 147,700 in Homs; 110,000 hectares in Hama; 83,000 in Idlib province; 62,000 in Damascus; 17,500 in Deir al-Zur; and less than 10,500 hectares in each of the remaining provinces. As these figures show, the predominantly Kurdish province of al-Hasakeh underwent the largest expropriation of land and surrounding northern provinces also saw more land expropriation than southern provinces.[31]

This expropriated land was intended to be redistributed amongst the rural population so that each beneficiary would not own more than 8 hectares of irrigated land or 45 hectares of non-irrigated land. Redistributed land could not be sold or rented and beneficiaries were required to work the land themselves.[32]

These land reforms had an overall negative impact. While those with traditional farming experience were able to work their land and benefit financially by not having to pay large landholders, those with little agricultural experience faced difficulties. Individuals with non-irrigated land struggled to provide for their family and instead had to seek alternative employment to support them. These problems in turn affected overall agricultural output in Syria.[33]

This movement of Kurds and Arabs with the result of altering the demographic makeup of a region bears a striking resemblance to points eight and nine of Lt Muhammad Talab Hilal's report. The movement also resulted in the effective separation and isolation of many Syrian Kurds from their counterparts in Turkey and Iraq, although it is arguable that a key reason for implementing the Arab Belt to separate Syria from Turkey and Iraq was due to conflict over water and a desire to pre-empt interference from Turkey or Iraq.

HAFIZ AL-ASAD

An 'Alawi military officer from Lataqiyya region, Hafiz al-Asad became commander of the Syrian Air Force in 1964 and was later made Minister of Defence in 1966 during Ba'th Party rule. Following his initial coup in 1970, al-Asad succeeded in retaining strict control over Syria until his death in 2000.[34] Today, his legacy can be seen throughout Syria in the streets and buildings named after him and the multiple images and memorials of al-Asad in every city. During his rule, al-Asad dominated the government, parliament, the Ba'th Party and civil society and made Syria in his own image, defining himself as father of Syria and an Arab hero who commanded the loyalty of his subjects.

Upon first assuming power, Hafiz al-Asad was seen by many as the antithesis of the previously unwanted regimes that had controlled Syria.[35] Instead, al-Asad redefined the nature of his Ba'th Party, the state and national institutions to consolidate his power and remove any challenge to his leadership, ensuring he could rule over Syria with an iron grip. He abandoned much of the extreme socialist language previously adopted by the Ba'th Party and instead sought to establish a broader support base with economic and political liberalizations.[36] State institutions were expanded, professionalized and consolidated and all domestic politics were moved within al-Asad's control. This power enabled him to establish Syria as a serious regional player rather than the object of stronger states' interests.[37]

In doing this, Hafiz al-Asad was cautious and prudent in his decision making, seeking to avoid taking risks both domestically and in the arena of foreign affairs. Knowing that his power depended on continuing loyalty from 'Alawi military supporters, he placed key supporters and family members in strategic positions within the military and the regime. To avoid allegations of sectarianism, al-Asad incorporated the Sunni majority and other minorities into the Ba'th Party and the government. However, al-Asad's personal ideals were Arabist in nature; he believed that Israel had humiliated Syria and other Arab countries in 1967. His foreign policy was affected by this belief, and one of his priorities was in strengthening the Arab countries' military positions in the struggle against Israel, despite the initial negative impact on his domestic goal of socialist transformation. Having obtained power largely on the concepts of national unity and Arab nationalism, al-Asad continued to use Arabist credentials and rhetoric. This deepened national divisions within Syria, especially between the Arabs and Kurds, causing the Kurds to be defined as a threat to national unity.

BASHAR AL-ASAD

Immediately following Hafiz al-Asad's death on 10 June 2000, the Syrian Constitution was amended such that the minimum age of presidential candidates became 34 instead of the previous 40. Bashar al-Asad, Hafiz's 34-year-old son, was nominated for the presidency soon after. A month later, on 10 July 2000, Bashar al-Asad was elected as Syria's president for a seven-year term following an unopposed referendum in which official statistics state that he obtained 97.29 per cent of the votes cast.

The assumption had always been that Bashar's older brother Basil al-Asad would become president after Hafiz and indeed, Basil had been groomed for many years by Hafiz to be ready for this succession. Basil's unexpected death in 1994 shifted Bashar into the position of key contender for the presidency.[38] Bashar had previously been living in London, pursuing a medical career and studying to become an ophthalmologist, when his career underwent a dramatic shift towards Syrian politics. Given his background, many in the West were hopeful of change and democratic reform, especially since Bashar had received limited military training, unlike his father and earlier Syrian leaders. Despite this external pressure for reform, little liberalization has been witnessed. What liberalization has occurred has been slow and mainly confined to Syria's economy. Little change has been seen within the political sphere, although whether the responsibility for stifling political reform lies with the staunch defenders of Hafiz al-Asad's executive policies or with Bashar himself is not yet clear.

Following Bashar al-Asad's inauguration, the inconsistencies between Syrian policy and domestic reform were rationalized as showing the power struggle between the 'old guard' and reformist 'new guard' with theories suggesting that Bashar was constrained by the 'old guard' who sought to retain their privileges and power. Over time, the view that Bashar's commitment to pan-Arab ideology is greater than suspected has begun to develop, particularly amongst the US administration.[39] However, an attempt to draw clear distinctions between an 'old' and 'new' guard is difficult because many of the interests of these groups overlap, thus trying to provide simple theories to explain the lack of political reform is unhelpful.[40]

Bashar himself, although educated in the West, received his political education from an entirely Ba'thist standpoint and holds a position of power that is dependent upon the regime which produced him.[41] At the same time, he is aware that economic reform has an inevitable effect on the stability of the state and the longevity of the regime.[42] Whether Bashar balances the different considerations and concludes that political reform is necessary remains to be seen, although increasing pressure for reform both internally and from external sources may assist him in drawing his conclusion.

Bashar al-Asad's inaugural speech indicated intent to reconcile the government and opposition,[43] and Bashar soon granted hitherto unseen levels of freedom of assembly to political activities and supporters.[44] But when Syrian opposition leaders and supporters attempted to benefit from this new freedom by holding discussions and debates that were often critical of the regime, Bashar's political authority was tested severely.

DAMASCUS SPRING

In early 2000, a civil society movement emerged that came to be known as the 'Damascus Spring'.[45] Political reform was encouraged though civil forums that were held in many places including private homes. Their hosts consisted of party leaders, members of parliament, journalist, lawyers, academics, businessmen, artists and philosophers, all of whom spoke on the need for political, economic and human rights reform and the underlying need for an autonomous civil society within Syria.[46] Independent human rights groups reopened, the Kurdish Jeladet Bedrakhan Cultural Association established itself in Qamishli and several hundred political prisoners were released up to May 2001. Hopeful of a newly free and open political system which could steer the country towards democracy, petitions were circulated and sent to the government, calling for reforms.[47]

By mid-2001, Bashar had responded. As early as March 2001, the Bedrakhan Cultural Association was closed and many of its members arrested.[48] Pioneers of the civil society movement were arrested along with other prominent human rights activists. Since then, many other activists have been arrested and civil forums in peoples' homes were declared illegal.[49]

Following elections for the people's Assembly in March 2003, Bashar al-Asad made a speech to open the new Assembly, delineating more clearly what he mean by the reform discussed in his inaugural speech. Bashar explained that the opposition had misunderstood his reference to democracy to mean freedom from control and morality, which was damaging to the national interest. Making clear that such activity would not be tolerated, Bashar set clear limits on future reform, indicating that reform will happen according to the authorities and not the people.

MARCH 2004 UNREST

On 12 March 2004, a football match in Qamishli, a town in northern Syria, set in motion a series of events from which many Kurds are still facing repercussions today. The buildup to the match, held between a local team and a team from Deiz Azour, involved the chanting of slogans with political connotations, which increased tension between supporters of both teams. Clashes eventually broke out and the security forces, instead of using tear gas and water hoses to dispel those fighting, intervened by opening fire on the unarmed supporters, killing at least seven Kurds and wounding many others as a result.

On 13 March 2004, funerals were held for those killed the previous day. Thousands of people attended, chanting political slogans and carrying Kurdish flags and pictures of Kurdish leaders to express their anger at what had occurred. Clashes broke out between these demonstrators and the police who again opened fire, killing and injuring more people and serving only to further increase people's agitation; this was then expressed by the vandalizing of buildings. People injured during these clashes were initially taken to several public and private hospitals in Qamishli for treatment, but were later transferred under police escort and held under intensive guard in the National Hospital. Despite requests from families to return the injured to private hospitals, only two people were in fact permitted to be transferred.

Following these incidents, dozens of Kurds living in Qamishli were arrested, regardless of whether they had been present at the demonstrations. Some of those arrested were children, including a 17-year-old who was released after nine days suffering from injuries reportedly sustained by torture. Even in April 2004, random arrests in Qamishli were still being reported.[50]

The unrest in Qamishli spread to other towns along the northern border of Syria, and also to Damascus and Aleppo. Between 12 and 13 March, Damascus University students demonstrated repeatedly against the events of Qamishli; on each occasion the police used force to try and stop the demonstration, causing students to respond. Hundreds of students were arrested both during and after the demonstrations and later expelled from the University. In the Wadie Al Mushareer area of Damascus, where a demonstration had also turned violent following police intervention, a meeting was held to try and reduce tension; instead, within hours of the meeting, 650 Kurds had been arrested.[51]

In total, at least 30 people were killed and 160 injured.[52] Despite relative calm having been restored to the region, the events served as a stark reminder of the significance of the Kurdish question to the Syrian government. Although comments by the government since March 2004 have suggested that the state will be more accommodating towards the Kurds, practical moves have yet to be made and Kurdish political and cultural activities are still affected.[53]

4
Syrian State Structure

THE POLITICAL SYSTEM

Article 1 of the Syrian Constitution describes Syria as a 'democratic, popular, socialist and sovereign state'. However, many facets of Syrian politics contradict this concept, as will be seen in this chapter.

Access to political power in Syria is highly selective, due to *wasta*, an Arabic term for personal connections. Syrian politics is underpinned by an intricate vertical patronage network and gaining admittance to this network requires connections to influential individuals or access to money with which to obtain influence and favours.

This concept of patronage has permeated throughout Syrian society, so that access to state benefits, employment, subsidies and other aspects of daily life often depends on an individual developing the appropriate connections. Although in theory anybody can develop such connections and benefit both socially and economically by gaining access to decision makers, access to such a network requires demonstrating loyalty to the Ba'th ideology and regime. The existence of social and economic benefits associated with showing such loyalty creates a disincentive to represent interests other than those approved by the Ba'thists and thus ensuring representation of minority groups such as the Kurds is difficult.

It is also impossible to speak of Syrian politics without referral to the military. Since Hafiz al-Asad's coup which he referred to as a 'Corrective Movement' in 1970,[1] mainstream politics has been permanently linked to the military. Coming from the military, al-Asad was able to ensconce the military firmly within Syrian politics at the expense of the civilian section of the Ba'th Party and military personnel now dominate the Party. Al-Asad then concentrated on strengthening and expanding the military, creating a new group of Syrians with a personal interest in maintaining the status quo. The military thus came to represent a means to an end for those seeking a rise in personal status or for minority group members seeking protection from the Sunni majority.

In strengthening the military, Hafiz al-Asad placed loyal and predominantly 'Alawi officers in strategic positions within both the armed forces and Syrian intelligence. This policy insured al-Asad against further military coups and reduced future threats to the regime. In doing this, Hafiz al-Asad finally achieved what others had attempted ever since the first military coup of 1949 – to stabilize and neutralize the military, preventing it from posing the constant threat to regime change that it had posed until 1970. Crediting al-Asad with the stabilization of Syria's political climate cannot however occur without noting the cost of this achievement: the military and intelligence services provide much of the regime's domestic controls and the brutality of both institutions has been starkly displayed on many occasions.

In the 1970s, a variety of factors contributed to a building unrest within Syria. The opposition occurred due to the state of the Syrian economy, the 1976 invasion of Lebanon by Syrian forces and the increasing belief that the Ba'th Party was a predominantly 'Alawi faction. Marxists, communists, professionals and human rights activists began to contest Ba'th Party rule, as did the Syrian Muslim Brotherhood. The Ba'th regime worked to suppress uprisings and increasingly targeted the Muslim Brotherhood, passing Law No. 49 on 7 July 1980, according to which mere membership of the Muslim Brotherhood warranted a death sentence.

On 27 July 1980, hundreds of detained Brotherhood members were killed in a military attack on Tadmur Prison. On 2 February 1982, Syrian forces were dispersed to the city of Hama, a known stronghold of the Muslim Brotherhood. After laying siege to the city with artillery and shelling, armed and special forces then stormed through the city, ransacking property and punishing civilians.[2] After 27 days, thousands of citizens had been killed and thousands more made homeless due to the destruction of a third of the city. Women, children and the elderly were among the victims.[3]

This display of military force appears to have occurred with the full support of al-Asad's government. According to the Syrian Human Rights Committee, the campaign against Hama was led by Rifa'at Asad, younger brother to Hafiz al-Asad who became martial ruler of northern and central districts of Syria two months earlier.[4] Such a clear demonstration of force was highly effective in silencing the burgeoning political opposition. The use of such a level of violence has not been seen again, although it has been used to a lesser extent to subdue sectarian discord. During the March 2004 protests in Qamishli, the use of force resulted in the death of approximately 30 Kurds and the detention of hundreds more.[5]

Following the events of Hama, al-Asad further increased the size of the Syrian military, forming multiple groups with the task of gathering intelligence. These often-competing groups control all aspects of movement and society, effectively restricting freedom of expression by instilling a fear within the general population of being informed on and the possible consequences.

The Syrian Arab Socialist Ba'th Party

The Ba'th Party has been the ruling party in Syria since 1963, although it was established in 1947. Its socialist, secular nature attracted previously marginalized sections of Syrian society, particularly minority groups and its accompanying Arab ideology was welcomed by them. Unlike traditional methods of obtaining political power, the Party followed a method of recruiting support from minority groups and building up its military strength through these groups. Its membership of a few hundred in 1963 grew to 8,000 by 1966 and 65,000 by 1971. By 1992, membership was estimated at 1 million.[6] This growth in membership may be due to the popularity of the Party or a simple reflection of the fact that membership offers many political and financial privileges. Anybody can join the Ba'th Party, on condition that they accept the goal of Arab unity. For many minority groups, the compromise on their ethnic identity is often worth the political support and additional benefits they obtain upon joining.

The Ba'th Party slogan, today found in the Constitution, is 'Unity, freedom, and socialism'. 'Unity' stands more specifically for 'Arab unity' and according to the Constitution the Party is dedicated to taking all necessary steps to achieve decentralized administration for all Arab states together with the administration of individual states by regional commands of the Ba'th Party itself.[7]

The reorganization of the Party in 1970 saw collective leadership replaced by an individual leader, Hafiz al-Asad. The changed structure requires that policy decisions are taken by the President and his key officials and then circulated throughout both the Party leadership and the national party membership.[8]

The Ba'th Party retains control of all Syrian political institutions. Under Article 8 of the Constitution, it is the leading party of the Republic and is responsible for directing the Progressive National Front in serving the interests of the Arab nation. The remaining parties within the Progressive National Front hold a limited political mandate, effectively freeing the Ba'th Party from competition. Within the Syrian Cabinet, membership is dominated by Ba'th Party ministers.

Ba'th Party Regional Command

The Regional Command is the political leadership of the Party, although much of its former power has been lost to the President and government.[9] The Regional Command is responsible for proposing the candidate for presidency to the Syrian parliament.[10]

Ba'th Party National Command

The National Command is the pan-Arab leadership of the Party. Technically, the National Command occupies a higher position than the Regional Command, but in practice, the National Command has become a subordinate to the Regional Command, representing little more than an 'honorary board'.[11]

The President of the Republic

Under Article 83 of the original Constitution, candidates for the Presidency of the Republic must be an Arab Syrian over the age of 40, although following the death of Hafiz al-Asad, the age requirement dropped to 34; conveniently, this was the precise age of Bashar al Asad.

Presidential elections are ordered by the People's Assembly following a proposal by the Arab Socialist Ba'th Party Regional Command and to win the election, a candidate requires an absolute majority of the votes.[12] As official statistics are not published to show the proportion of voter turnout during presidential elections, it is impossible to know whether 3, 50 or 99 per cent of the voting-age population actually turned out to cast their votes for Hafiz or Bashar al-Asad in recent years. If only 3 per cent of the population turned out to vote and all voted for the sole candidate standing for election, it is difficult to see how this truly meets the concept of a democratic absolute majority vote.

The Constitution states that a President then rules for a term of seven years. However, Article 71 of the Constitution states that the People's Assembly are responsible for nominating candidates to stand for the Presidency: as will be seen, all actions of the People's Assembly are governed by the Ba'th Party and thus the nominations are also governed by the Ba'th Party. As nobody has actually stood in opposition to Hafiz or Bashar al-Asad since the 1970 Corrective Movement, the concept that a President only runs for seven years before competing against others to return to power does not hold true. In reality, the accession of Hafiz al-Asad's son seems to represent a hereditary republic more than it does a democratic one: instead of succession being decided by properly democratic elections, it appears to have followed a dynastic line.[13]

The President of the Republic holds wide ranging powers. He can appoint and dismiss the Prime Minister, his deputies and other ministers. He appoints and dismisses civilian and military officials.[14] The President can also form specialized organizations, councils, and committees and specify their powers and jurisdiction. Furthermore, the President has the power to dissolve the People's Assembly.[15]

The President assumes responsibility for ensuring respect of the Constitution, the orderly functioning of public authorities, the preservation of the state and the exercising of executive authority on behalf of the people. In consultation with the Cabinet, he lays down the state's general policy and supervises its implementation.[16] The President promulgates laws approved by the People's Assembly and can veto these laws; he also issues decrees, decisions and orders in accordance with legislation.[17] In the interim period between People's Assemblies, the President assumes legislative authority and is not required to refer any of the legislation issued during this period to the next People's Assembly.[18]

The President is the supreme commander of the armed forces and is responsible for declaring and terminating a state of emergency within Syria.[19] In situations threatening national unity, the safety and independence of the homeland or situations obstructing state institutions from carrying out their constitutional responsibilities, the President can take immediate measures necessitated by these circumstances. In addition, if it is necessary in order to safeguard the country's national interests or the requirements of national security, the President can assume legislative authority although any legislation passed must be referred to the People's Assembly in its first session.[20]

The Council of Ministers / Cabinet

This consists of the Council President, his deputies and ministers, all of whom are responsible to the President of the Republic.[21] The Council supervises the execution of laws and regulations and the work of state institutions. It assists the President of the Republic in drawing up and carrying out the state's policy. Among other tasks, the Cabinet also prepares draft laws, follows up the enforcement of laws, ensures state security and issues executive and administrative decisions in accordance with laws and regulations.[22]

Majlis al-sha'ab: the Syrian Parliament or People's Assembly[23]

The first People's Assembly was appointed by Hafiz al-Asad in 1971 and the first elections were held in 1973. Since then, elections have been held every four years by secret ballot.[24] According to Article 52 of the Constitution, Assembly members represent the people and their mandate must not be restricted. Each member of the Assembly must take the oath specified in Article 7.[25]

Unlike a normal parliament which would be expected to carry out decision making, legislative functions and policy-related work, the Syrian People's Assembly carries out little more than a consultative role.[26] The Assembly is responsible for nominating the President of the Republic, approval of the laws, debate of cabinet policy, approval of budget and development plans, approval of international treaties and agreements, approval of general amnesty, acceptance or rejection of member resignations and the withholding of confidence in the Cabinet or a minister.[27] This is an extremely narrow mandate in comparison to that assigned to the executive and means that in practical terms, the Ba'th Party is the main decision-making body in Syria.

The number of members in the Assembly increased from 195 to 250 deputies in 1990, of which approximately one third of seats are reserved for independent candidates and the remainder for parties within the Progressive National Front.

The Progressive National Front

Upon obtaining control of Syria, one of the Ba'th Party's main tactics for neutralizing political rivals was to create the Progressive National Front (PNF, or the Front) and designate it as the official area of Syrian politics. Parties that comprise the PNF are the only parties legally permitted to exist in Syria. To join the PNF, a party was required to accept the Ba'th Party programme, and as leader of the Front, the Ba'th Party ensured it was guaranteed a majority in all its bodies.[28] Today, the Progressive National Front comprises seven parties including the Ba'th Party.

The PNF has a variety of tasks and aims. In furtherance of Article 8 of the Syrian Constitution, the Front mobilizes the capacity of the masses in order to further objectives of the Arab nation. The Front aims to liberate occupied Arab territories, decide on questions of war and peace and to formulate economic, social, cultural, political and military plans for Syria. The Front must also further the cultural, social and political development of Syrian citizens. The Front is responsible for establishing a system of popular democracy with constitutional institutions and local councils, in order to ensure the full sovereignty of the people. The Front is tasked with development of the democratic structure of popular and occupational organizations, by providing them with all possible means to play their role in ensuring the people's control over executive organs. Finally, the PNF approves Ba'th Party five-year plans.[29]

By accepting Ba'th Party ideology and policy in order to join the PNF, it is difficult to see that any of the seven parties are truly independent. In Volker Perthes' words,

> The front stands for a system that basically denies the existence of political conflict, and thereby restricts the chances for their political settlement by competition, that is, open debate, negotiation and compromise.[30]

Perthes considers that only two of the parties within the PNF are truly political parties in their own right: the Syrian Communist Party (SCP) and the Ba'th Party itself.

Until legislative changes, all members of the People's Assembly were also members of a PNF party, with a majority of Assembly members being from the Ba'th Party; now one third of Assembly seats are reserved for independent candidates.[31] This body cannot initiate laws or make policy decisions, but its views on economic matters are considered by policy-makers.

Beyond the Progressive National Front, the existence of any other political party is forbidden by law. Activity by illegal parties is generally tolerated if the party ideology and political views do not openly conflict with Ba'th policy and if party activities remain in the private sphere. Although independent candidates can now run for election to the People's Assembly, any potential candidate must be approved by the authorities,[32] requiring that they do not challenge the Ba'th Party ideology or abstain from promoting any agenda other than that endorsed by the Ba'th Party.

The Syrian Ba'th Party has been extremely successful in the neutralization of rivals both by forcing them to accept Ba'th ideology and by fragmenting party membership through the auspices of the PNF. Instead of parties combining to challenge the Ba'th political agenda, loyalties are divided and internal dissent makes it difficult to form a coherent opposition.

Popular organizations

Under Ba'th Party rule popular organizations, which many people join in order to find employment, have sprung up throughout Syria.[33] Such organizations include the Trade Union, Peasants Union, Women's Union, the National Union of Students and the Revolutionary Youth Organisation. These organisations are under Ba'th Party authority, forming part of the Syrian hierarchical state system and providing a method by which the Party can control and enforce loyalty to the state.[34] The popular organizations were brought under the authority of the Ba'th Party in 1976, following the general unrest of the 1970s during which several organizations became involved with democracy activists.

THE ECONOMIC SYSTEM

The combination of several events in the 1980s led to economic crisis for Syria. Oil prices plummeted due to a worldwide glut in production, both reducing Syria's export revenues but also reducing the financial aid given to them by other oil-rich countries. In the agricultural sector, a severe ten-year drought had caused devastation to the industry. Finally, as the Cold War began to wind down, so did the economic aid that Syria had formerly been receiving from the Soviet Union.

This crisis made it clear that a more investor-friendly business environment was required in Syria, in order to attract foreign investment and repair the economy. Several decrees were passed between 1985 and 1991 which were designed to increase foreign investment, provide more freedom to the private sector and clamp down on corruption.

However, the liberalization and stabilization that al-Asad intended to achieve by such decrees was selective. Al-Asad knew that if he permitted uncontrolled liberalization, this would undermine the system of public patronage that was keeping his regime in power. This concern has meant that Syria's economic reforms have been based on the political motives of regime survival and regional standing.[35]

With a GDP of $21.5 billion in 2003 and a per capita income of $1,020, the World Bank classes Syria as a lower middle-income economy. Oil and agriculture provide the majority of Syria's revenue, with large oil discoveries accounting for healthy economic growth between 1990 and 1995. However, Syria's oil reserves are only expected to last a further twelve years based on the current extraction rate and new discoveries of oil are likely to extend this by only another five to eight years at most, although this may be offset against the development of natural gas production. In addition, the economic growth of the early 1990s has not been maintained, and despite major economic reform, the Syrian economy remains weak.[36] The World Bank cites a growth rate of 2.5 per cent for 2003.[37]

Syrian unemployment currently stands at approximately 20 per cent of the labour force and the Syrian education system has been criticized for failing to provide both a good quality of education and economically relevant skills. The US Department of State estimates that almost 60 per cent of the population is under the age of 20.[38] The World Bank classes Syria's main challenge as being

> To achieve sustainable high rates of growth to generate employment for a rapidly growing labor force ... If the youth's labor participation stays at the current 60 per cent rate, between 240,000 and 300,000 people will enter the labor force every year over the next 10 years ... The GDP necessary to absorb these new entrants to the labor force and to reduce existing unemployment is estimated to be around 8 per cent per year.[39]

The government has recently attempted to address structural deficiencies in the economy. For example, to resolve the lack of a modern financial sector, private banking was legalized in 2001 and by 2004, four private banks were operating. The Syrian government has also introduced changes to many tax laws and is reported to be considering similar changes in other areas. Interest rates were lowered for the first time in 22 years in 2003, and again in 2004. Some basic commodities continue to be heavily subsidized.[40]

In 2001, Syria also submitted a request to the World Trade Organization to begin the accession process and become part of the global economy. In order to join the WTO however, Syria would be required to change many of its trade rules.[41] The completion of an Association Agreement with the European Union will also have an impact on Syria's economy, providing trade liberalization.

At present, approximately 62,000 square kilometres of Syria's land is arable. Around 80 per cent of cultivated land depends on rainfall and following drought in the 1990s, the agricultural sector has finally begun to recover. Syrian priorities have shifted from the expansion of industry to the agricultural sector, which has transformed the country

from an importer of agricultural produce to an exporter of cotton,
fruits, vegetables and other foodstuffs. This shift was brought about
mainly by the Syrian government's investment in large irrigation
schemes in northern and north-eastern Syria, which it hopes will
increase irrigated farmland by 38 per cent over the next decade. This
is intended to achieve food self-sufficiency, reduce rural migration
and increase Syria's export income.[42]

Recent Syrian oil production stands at 530,000 barrels per day;
this includes both heavy grade oil and light grade low-sulphur oil.
Income from petroleum accounts for a large part of Syrian export
income, and work to develop its natural gas reserves for both domestic
use and export has also begun in conjunction with international
energy companies.[43]

Syria owes a large amount in foreign debt, although it has achieved
bilateral rescheduling deals with virtually all European creditors.[44]
However, its debt burden was an estimated $20.8 billion in 2001.[45]

THE LEGAL SYSTEM

The Syrian legal system is based on a combination of Islamic *sharia'*
law and civil law. Whilst French law forms the basis for much
of Syria's civil, commercial and criminal codes, *sharia'* is used to
determine issues of personal status, including marriage, divorce,
paternity custody of children and inheritance, although the *sharia'*
applied in Syria has been modified to provide a slightly improved
status for women.[46]

The Constitution

The current Syrian Constitution was introduced on 13 March 1973.
In its preamble, Syria is described as a region of the Arab homeland
and the government and independence of state are described
as 'instruments' to 'serve the struggle for the construction of the
United Socialist Arab society'[47] and the 'Arab nations comprehensive
unity'.[48] The Constitution professes a dedication to popular
democracy[49] and the principles of equity and freedom of expression
and universal education.[50]

The Constitution makes clear that all of its stipulations are subject
to the law. However, the state of emergency that has existed since
1962 overrides much of the Constitution, preventing its provisions
from being fully implemented and as a consequence preventing many

of the constitutional guarantees of freedom and protection of human rights from being upheld.

The state of emergency

The law establishing a state of emergency was declared in 1962 by the government that was in place immediately prior to the Ba'th Party coup.[51] On 8 March 1963, following the coup, Military Order No.2 reissued the state of emergency. This state of emergency has continued to the present day, thus by proxy it can be considered the basis for the Syrian legal framework, having existed for 40 years. The original state of emergency was not debated or agreed by the People's Assembly.[52] Within the Syrian Constitution, Article 113 legitimizes the state of emergency, permitting the President to take immediate unspecified measures necessitated by the circumstances to face the danger. The unspecified nature of these measures gives the president and his delegates a *carte blanche* to suppress domestic dissent.

State of emergency laws provide the President and his deputies with sweeping powers that can affect all areas of life. Opposition can be suppressed, freedom of movement and assembly restricted, media organizations can be closed down, mail can be censored and property confiscated or requisitioned.[53] Preventative arrest and denial of rights are permitted, as is the referral of individuals to military courts for 'offences against public authority', 'offences which disturb public confidence' or for those who 'constitute a general danger'.[54]

In essence, state of emergency provisions permit government institutions to act against any of the Syrian population without justification or reason and without fear of censure. Emergency laws are placed above state law, causing the overlap of executive, legislative and judicial powers and placing all three powers in the hand of the Martial Law Governor. This translates to a reality in which basic freedoms are denied or curtailed and arbitrary arrest and intimidation, detention without trial, torture and the disappearance of individuals are not uncommon. The law grants extraordinary powers of arrest and detention to the Military Governor (currently the President), powers which he delegates to the Syrian security services.[55] There are presently several hundred political prisoners being held without trial in Syria and individuals can be arrested on a variety of political charges including reading non-Ba'thist political material.[56] Many hundreds of Kurds were arrested following the events in Qamishli in March 2004, although few were charged with offences and many others have remained in detention for almost a year before standing trial.[57]

Such punishment of individuals for what might be considered day to day activities in the West ensures that opposition movements and leaders rarely gain wide popular support.

The judicial authority

According to the Constitution, the judicial authority's independence is guaranteed by the President of the Republic with the assistance of the Higher Council of the Judiciary.[58] The Higher Council of the Judiciary is presided over by the President of the Republic.[59] Terms of appointment, promotion, transfer, discipline and dismissal of judges are defined by law.[60]

The Supreme Constitutional Court consists of five members, all of whom are appointed by the President of the Republic.[61] The Constitutional Court decides on the constitutionality of laws.[62] At the request of the President, the Constitutional Court also gives its opinion on the constitutionality of bills, legislative decrees and draft decrees.[63]

Although the Constitution envisages an independent judiciary,[64] this is far from the reality. In his role as Chairman of the High Judicial Council, the President plays a role in appointing and dismissing judges; he also has considerable power in forming and executing the law. It is very difficult to state with conviction that a judiciary is independent when the country's president heads the supreme court, holds considerable influence over the development of the law and provides little freedom for judges to interpret the law.

During the increasing oppositional activity of the late 1970s, the Lawyers Unions and Bar Association of Syria had played a leading role.[65] In response, the Syrian parliament dissolved many popular organizations for the reason that they had been '"infiltrated by reactionary elements" and were dangerous to society'.[66] Local and regional bars were closed and law No.39 of August 1981 ordered a complete reform of the bar. This reform brought the Lawyers Unions and Bar Association under Ba'th Party control, preventing democratic opposition members from gaining control or influence over other members.

Individuals arrested on political charges are generally tried before the Supreme Court, Constitutional Court or State Security Court. Syria's State Security Courts were established under the state of emergency and have been heavily criticized. Defendants have no rights of appeal against the decisions of the SSSC or military courts and routinely defence lawyers are denied access to their clients and/or denied adequate time for the preparation of their defence cases. As a result, thousands of political prisoners occupy the cells of Syrian jails serving undetermined sentences. Kurdish political and cultural activists commonly undergo Security Court proceedings for charges such as being members of illegal organizations and for separatism. Many of the hundreds of Kurds who have been arrested or detained since the Kurdish unrest in March 2004, are unlikely to appear before a court or receive any public attention.

The state of the Syrian legal system and redundancy of judicial proceedings have caused many lawyers to leave the legal profession.

The Penal Code

The Syrian Penal Code provides guarantees against abuse of authority and obstruction of the law; guarantees freedom of association, expression and assembly; and provides guarantees against any form of torture.[67] Article 307 of the same Penal Code provides for the crimes of instigating confessional or racial bigotry or provoking conflict among the various communities and component elements of the nation; Article 308 provides for the crime of membership of any association established with the purposes referred to in Article 307.[68] Both clauses are often used against sectors in society who do not follow the Arab nation party line, particularly the Kurds.

The procedure for passing new laws in Syria requires the submission of draft bills to parliament for discussion, providing an opportunity for parliament to suggest amendments with the government. Parliament then votes on the draft bill after which it is resubmitted to the President. The President may then promulgate the bill, send it back to parliament or veto it.[69] Although in theory a Presidential veto can be overruled by a two thirds majority in parliament, this has never happened.[70]

5
Regional Relations

Regional relations play their role in the situation of the Kurds in Syria and in other states. As well as the individual state interests that have affected the Syrian authorities' treatment of its Kurdish population, regional rivalries and cooperation have impacted on efforts to find a just solution to the Kurdish question. The *realpolitik* of state politics together with the international borders that split the Kurds between several states have linked the foreign and domestic policies of all these states. As a consequence of this, Kurdish groups have resorted to exploiting regional rivalries in order to serve their own interests within a specific state; meanwhile the Kurds themselves have been used as pawns in individual states' foreign policies, according to the geopolitical and strategic interests of the regional state concerned.

The reported cooperation between states such as Syria, Turkey and Iraq on the Kurdish 'problem' has aimed to weaken the Kurdish movement throughout Kurdistan and prevent the establishment of any form of independent Kurdish state or autonomous region.[1] The extent to which these countries coordinate their policies and strategies towards the Kurds is unclear to external observers, because the regular meetings between these states are not public. However, similar tactics are used in each state to prevent Kurdish political, economic and social organization and activity. In each country, Kurds have been subjected to language restrictions and prohibited from practising their culture and traditions. They have undergone forced and artificial demographic change and been the subject of discriminatory laws.

On occasion, many states have lent support to the Kurdish movements of neighbouring states when it suited their own interests. Syria's history of hostile relations with Iraq and Turkey has seen the Kurds used frequently as pawns between the three governments to achieve strategic aims. The Kurds of Iraq gained support from the Shah of Iran in the 1970s prior to the Algiers Agreement of 1975, and gained support from Syria due to Syrian–Iraqi Ba'th party rivalry. Both Iran and Syria have in the past also supported the Kurds in Turkey. This strategic importance of the Kurds to each of the powerful Middle

Eastern states has caused Kurdish politics to become complicated by inter-state interests, relations and strategy. However, at the same time the Kurds themselves, particularly the Kurds of Iraq, have been able to exploit these inter-state rivalries to gain support for their political or armed struggles.

Syrian domestic state affairs and the interests of Kurds in Syria are heavily affected by the domestic affairs of Turkey and Iraq, both of which have large Kurdish populations. Most recently, hostilities between Syria, Turkey and Iran have been overridden by the 2003 Iraq War and the events that have followed. Fear that the Kurds in Iraq may incite increased Kurdish demands for autonomy within neighbouring countries has led to renewed anti-Kurdish policy throughout these countries. Consequently, the heightened problems experienced by the Kurds in Syria over recent years can only be understood in the context of the war on terror, the Iraq War and the way in which these two campaigns have affected Syria, its neighbour and their relations to each other. Although these events have had profound consequences across the Middle East, Syria has been particularly affected, given its Arab Ba'thist ideology and vulnerability to external regional and international pressures.

TURKEY

Overall, Syrian–Turkish relations have historically been strained, but recent events have improved relations between the two countries.

During the French Mandate, Hatay province, a coastal area to the west of Syria and north of Lebanon, was ceded/given to Turkey by the French in exchange for which Ankara signed a non-aggression treaty with the Mandate powers. Syria has always considered this land to have been unjustly partitioned and continues to define Hatay province as occupied Syrian territory. In addition, Syrian–Turkish relations have been strained by Turkey's activities along the Euphrates and Tigris rivers, both of which flow from Turkey into Syria, and then to Iraq. Issues of water sharing between Turkey, Syria and Iraq are discussed in the next chapter.

Syria and Turkey have also conflicted over Israel, with whom Turkey has enjoyed low-level relations concentrating on bilateral trade, agriculture and intelligence for many years. In 1996, wide-ranging economic agreements expanded Turkish–Israeli relations to economic ties, strategic consultation and military cooperation. This 1996 cooperation was based on the common 'terrorist threat' that both countries faced from the Kurds in Turkey's south-east and the Palestinians in Israel.[2] Syrian unease stemmed from the potential military threats and strategic encirclement posed by this relationship, together with concerns over future control of the Euphrates River. Israeli private investment in Turkey's GAP project caused the Syrian Defence Minister to accuse Israel of using Turkey and the Euphrates to pressure Syria into concessions with Israel.[3]

In the early 1980s, Abdullah Öcalan and members of the *Partîya Karkerên Kurdistan* (PKK) entered Syria, where they established PKK offices and training camps in both Damascus and the Beqaa Valley, Lebanon. The organization expanded and by 1984 was reportedly using its bases in Syria and Lebanon from which to launch armed attacks on Turkey.

The presence of the PKK in Syria was tolerated by the Syrian authorities for political reasons. In permitting the PKK to stay on Syrian soil and carry out activities, Syria could apply pressure on Turkey and thus balance out the advantage held by Turkey over Syria in relation to control of the Euphrates water flows. At the same time, Turkey used its control over water flows to pressure Syria regarding PKK activities within Syrian territory.

Relations between the two countries had deteriorated to the point that each country had assembled troops on respective sides of the Turkish–Syrian border by late 1998. However, once Syria agreed to expel Abdullah Öcalan, the crisis was averted. Since Syria and Turkey signed the Adana Agreement in 1998 under which Syria agreed not to foster relations with the PKK or facilitate their activities in any way, hostilities between the two countries have eased. The 2003 Iraq War and resulting question on the future of Iraqi Kurdistan have further increased cooperation between Syria and Turkey and in January 2004, Bashar al-Asad became the first Syrian head of state to visit Turkey. Following al-Asad's visit, the two countries agreed further cooperation on terrorism and extradition issues, as a result of which many Kurds have been returned to Turkey from Syria.[4]

Despite palpable differences in the methods adopted by each state (in that Syria has neither undertaken military suppression of its Kurdish population nor destroyed Kurdish towns and villages), Turkish and Syrian policies regarding the Kurds are similar. Forced assimilation and engineered demographic change have occurred in both countries, due to an inability to accept the Kurdish national identity. Recent Turkish and Syrian foreign and domestic policy has been heavily influenced by considerations preventing the creation of a Kurdish state or autonomous area. During the buildup to the 2003 Iraq War, Syria opposed military action against Iraq and instead stood in support of the Ba'thist regime, a regime that Syria has historically been hostile towards. At the same time, Turkey risked its relationship with both the US and the EU by refusing the US access to southern Turkey in order to send US troops into northern Iraq.

Turkey and Syria's split with foreign policy occurred due to concerns over the potential after-effects of an end to the Ba'thist regime in Iraq. The inevitable international interest in the Kurdish question and its resultant effect on regional dynamics meant that both countries' interests were best served firstly by opposing the initial war on Iraq and trying to maintain the status quo; then by insisting on the preservation of Iraq's territorial integrity and so removing the possibility of a permanent Kurdish autonomous region; and finally by opposing all attempts at allowing the Iraqi Kurds to retain any regional control. Both countries fear the potential effects of any Kurdish gains on their own minority Kurdish populations and this fear has caused Syria and Turkey to close ranks like never before.

IRAQ

Despite coming to power in both countries in 1963, the two Ba'th Party branches have competed over the true interpretation of Ba'th ideology and for regional Arab leadership. After Syria sided with Iran in the Iraq–Iran War of 1980–88, relations with Iraq were almost completely severed. It was not until 1997 that the two countries began meaningful cooperation, a process that has gathered increased momentum since the accession of Bashar al-Asad.

Tensions also developed between the two countries because of depleting water reserves and Turkish and Syrian control of downstream water supplies to Iraq. Tensions peaked in 1973 as Syria completed construction of the Tabqa Dam and began to fill Lake Asad reducing the flow of the Euphrates to a trickle. In 1995 Iraq accused Syria of holding back water and called for intervention from the Arab League. By the end of May that year conflict over the Tabqa Dam and water flows brought Syria and Iraq to the brink of war. With Saudi mediation an unofficial agreement was reached where Syria would keep 40 per cent of water and allow 60 per cent to flow into Iraq. Tensions were also caused when Turkey began to fill the Ataturk Dam in 1990. Syria and Iraq accused Turkey of not informing them that the water would be cut off and Iraq threatened to bomb Euphrates dams. Again the next chapter discusses conflict over water resources between Syria, Turkey and Iraq in greater detail.

Gulf War

As the first Gulf War came to an end in early 1991 and Iraqi forces withdrew from Kuwait, American rhetoric encouraged the Iraqi people to take matters into their own hands. Believing that they would receive US support, popular uprisings began to spread throughout Iraq in March 1991. However, when the US failed to provide support to the Shi'i Muslims in the south and the Kurds in the north, Saddam Hussein's forces intervened to subdue the revolt.

From 28 March 1991, the Kurdish regions of northern Iraq experienced devastating military assaults by the Iraqi Ba'thist regime. This harsh suppression, combined with memories of the recent Anfal campaign and chemical attacks on Halabja during the Iraq–Iran War, caused many thousands of Kurds to flee into Turkey and Iran; within 48 hours of the military assault commencing, approximately 1.85 million Kurds had fled the region, some pouring into Turkey and Iran, others remaining in Iraq's mountainous border regions.[5]

Both Turkey and Iran were overwhelmed with the magnitude of refugees. Turkey's immediate concerns over the effect of a sudden influx of Iraqi Kurdish refugees into its own Kurdish regions, prompted it to close its borders and refuse asylum to Iraqi Kurds. This combination of a lack of preparation, the closure of the Turkish border and Turkey's refusal to permit UN humanitarian assistance to the Iraqi Kurds within its territory, along with harsh weather conditions and an ill-equipped refugee population, contributed to a humanitarian crisis in which up to 1,000 refugees per day began to die of cold, disease and starvation.[6]

Given momentum by the urgent humanitarian situation, the international community began to act. Initially suggested by Turkey in an attempt to relieve the pressure on its borders and prevent Iraqi Kurds from fomenting resistance within its own sensitive Kurdish areas, on 5 April 1991 UN Resolution 688 was adopted, providing for the establishment of a 'safe haven' in northern Iraq. The Resolution declared that the internal repression of Iraqi citizens was a threat to peace and security in the region and authorized UN action to prevent such repression and to provide humanitarian assistance within Iraqi territory.[7] UN action resulted in the creation of the 'safe haven' (with a UN-controlled border) in northern Iraq, the development of a Kurdish autonomous area, the withdrawal of Iraqi forces and the establishment of a 'no-fly' zone over the area.

Following the establishment of the 'safe haven' and the withdrawal of central Iraqi administration and control, elections were held in May 1992 which saw votes split almost equally between the KDP and PUK (the two major Kurdish political parties). Massoud Barzani and Jalal Talabani, leaders of the two parties, agreed on joint rule within the newly appointed Kurdistan Regional Government, although control was divided regionally and ideologically according to the location of their respective supporters. By 1994, fighting had broken out between the two parties along personal, political and economic lines; the tension had intensified to such an extent by 1996 that the KDP called for assistance from Baghdad and the PUK invited Iranian forces into PUK-controlled areas.[8]

Cooperation agreements in 1998 resolved the hostility and ended the sporadic civil violence in Iraqi Kurdistan, both parties agreeing not to seek external assistance or violence as a means of solving future disputes.[9] By the time Saddam Hussein's regime fell in 2003, the Kurdish politicians were thus in a strong position to form a part of the interim government. Their contribution to discussion on the future of Iraq has caused considerable unease both internally within Iraq and externally in Syria, Turkey and Iran.

The 2003 war on Iraq

The 2003 Iraq War saw the beginning of US redefinition of the Middle Eastern status quo, with consequent effects on Syria. Regime change, the presence of US troops and questions surrounding Iraq's social, economic and political future were all events at odds with Syria's internal and external objectives. Syria now perceives that the US military presence and support of the present Iraqi regime pose a direct threat to Syria's own regime and security.

More concerning for Syria is the prospect of a permanent Kurdish state in northern Iraq and its resultant effect on Syria's Kurdish population and the general precedent that dividing a sovereign state's territory would set. Iraq's reorganization could spark repercussions within Syria, with demands for separation, increased national rights or devolution of power.

2005 election

The Iraqi elections on 31 January 2005 saw a turnout of 8.5 million Iraqis, 58 per cent of registered voters. Within the Kurdish regions of northern Iraq, turnout was far higher than 58 per cent, with reports of between 80 and 90 per cent turnout in many areas.

The elections were held to appoint members of the new National Assembly, which was tasked with drafting a new Iraqi constitution. The 275 seats available on the Assembly were to be divided on a proportional representation basis, after voters had selected their chosen parties. Conscious of the need to obtain as many votes as possible to ensure good standing in the final results, the KDP and PUK joined together and ran as a Kurdish coalition. Since the election, the two Kurdish parties have agreed that Jalal Talabani, leader of the PUK, should be the person to represent both parties in any government. Talabani was a lieutenant under Mullah Mustafa Barzani who founded the KDP that is now led by Massoud Barzani. Talabani separated from the KDP in 1974 and formed the PUK in Damascus in 1975.

According to official results, 47.6 per cent of the vote went to an alliance of Shi'ite Islamist groups. The Kurdish coalition received 25.4 per cent of votes. As a result, 140 seats on the National Assembly went to the Shi'ite collation and 75 seats to the Kurdish collation. Forty seats went to Iyad Allawi's party and the remaining 20 seats to a mixture of other groups. The Kurds therefore comprise the second highest majority in the Assembly.

Within Kirkuk, the Kurds won nearly 60 per cent of the vote, which may result in controversial debates over the future of the city. Although the Kurds view Kirkuk as the capital of the Kurdish region, Turkomen and Arabs living in Kirkuk are fiercely opposed to such a possibility. Turkey has also made its feelings clear in a press release following the election results, alleging that there were irregularities in Kirkuk due to 'manipulations' and that 'certain elements of the Iraqi society attempted to manipulate the voting procedure and extracted illegal gains out of this practice'.[10]

It is anticipated that the Kurds will attempt to secure as much power under the proposed federal Iraq as possible. It is also expected that, when the National Assembly begins to draft the new Iraqi constitution, the Kurds will negotiate for as much autonomy as they can get. This is likely to increase local tensions between Syria, Turkey and Iraq as each country fears further claims for autonomy from their own Kurdish population.

Iraqi Kurdistan

The Syrian government was not initially opposed to the safe haven in northern Iraq. The safe haven weakened Baghdad but was still dependent on the goodwill of neighbouring countries to allow its population access to the outside world and was thus viewed as not posing any real threat to Syrian interests. The regional balance of power shifted in Syria's favour with the creation of the safe haven because US and Allied forces no longer needed to remain in the region following Saddam Hussein's withdrawal from Kuwait. With no international recognition and no Western input into the safe haven's future status, neither the Syrian nor Turkish governments felt concerned over the possibility of the situation changing in Iraq and Iraqi Kurdistan. Syria was consequently open about its relations with the Kurdish parties of northern Iraq and opened its borders to their political representatives and diplomats.

Events thus brought the Iraqi Kurdish political parties and Syrian authorities into a strategic relationship. However, this relationship has been two-sided because the Iraqi Kurds and the disputed status of Iraqi Kurdistan remain an area of concern for the Syrian authorities.

Due to its neutral perspective on Iraqi Kurdistan, Syria developed good relations with Iraqi Kurdish political parties, who provided an opportunity for the Syrians to apply pressure on Iraq's Ba'th regime. Both the KDP and PUK were permitted to open offices in Syria, which further benefited Syria by deflecting attention away from its internal Kurdish issues and instead redirecting attention to Iraqi Kurdish issues, weakening the Kurdish movement in Syria in the process. As they had with the PKK in Turkey, the Kurds in Syria provided much support to the Iraqi Kurdish movement at the expense of creating their own national movement. Already worried about the possibility of sectarian and ethnic strife within Syria and the influence that the development of a recognized and powerful Kurdish authority in northern Iraq might have on its own Kurdish population, Syria's concerns over the status and power of the Kurdish groups protected by the safe haven in northern Iraq, were increased by the threat of US-led intervention in Iraq against Saddam Hussein and the Ba'thist regime. The fear of any increase in power of the Iraqi Kurds has played on the mind of the government and has been a significant factor informing both domestic and foreign policies. This concern played a large part in influencing Syria to support Saddam Hussein and the Ba'th Party, condemning the Kurds and their alliance with the US-led forces.

Both leading Kurdish political parties of Iraqi Kurdistan maintain a policy of non-interference in the domestic affairs of neighbouring states. Although they have unofficial relations with the parties and the communities of Syria they are not active among the Kurdish population of Syria, nor do they support any political movement in Syria and rarely speak out on their behalf. Yet, the strength and standing of the KDP and PUK across Kurdistan mean that events in Iraq and Turkey naturally have some impact on the political aspirations of the Syrian Kurds.

At the same time, the establishment of a Kurdish-governed autonomous region gave hope to Kurds throughout the region, marking a shift in attitudes to the Kurdish question amongst the Kurds themselves and raising the possibility of improving their standing within individual states. It was inevitable that the confidence gained by Kurdish organizations, although initially focused towards the struggles of Kurds within Iraq, would eventually lead to political activity within Syria on the shortcomings of the Syrian state. Recent events have further stimulated this activity, but in response the Syrian state has clamped down more than ever on the Kurds within its borders.

Relations between the Kurds of Iraq and the Syrian regime have also been soured by the rise of Arab nationalist rhetoric and political opposition to proposals for formal federalism in Iraq and the self-government of the Kurdish areas. Although the Syrian authorities maintained relations with the Iraqi Kurdish parties and with individual members of the Iraqi Interim Governing Council, Syrian domestic affairs suggest that these two bodies represent a growing concern for Damascus.

With the war in Iraq and the involvement of the Kurds in aiding the occupied forces there, Kurds have become increasingly seen to be enemies and have been targeted as traitors. The fires of popular Arab nationalism have been fed by what is regarded as Western imperialist intervention in the Middle East and occupation of Iraq. The period since the war in Iraq has witnessed an increase in the numbers of Kurds arrested in Syria and detained for both political and cultural reasons. With the association of Kurds with the US-led alliance and invasion of Iraq, the evidence suggests that the Kurds in Syria have likewise been tainted by association. Today, more than ever, the Kurds of Iraq are seen by Damascus as a threat to Syria's internal stability, unity and security.

6
Water Resources and Conflict

'Conflict over transboundary rivers usually results from a power imbalance amongst riparians where one State or Province is sufficiently influential to exert its authority over others. Generally, upstream States are considered to be in a more influential position as they can control the water source, but regional power imbalances may make it possible for downstream riparians to exert influence over upstream States. Similar conflicts also occur within States where rivers cross internal political borders.'

World Commission on Dams (WCD)

'It is only with dams that states can significantly re-direct, store and otherwise alter the course of rivers to the extent that would cause changes of conflict-invoking proportions in neighbouring states.'

Fiona Curtin, consultant to the WCD[1]

THE EUPHRATES RIVER[2]

The Euphrates River originates in the mountains of north-east Turkey, where several tributaries rise before merging near Keban to form the Euphrates River itself. After Keban, the river flows south, crossing into Syria at Jarablus. Within Syria, it is joined by the Sajur and Balikh rivers before entering Iraq at Al'Qa'em. It finally joins the Tigris in the south of Iraq to form the Shatt Al-Arab River, which drains into the Arabian Gulf near Al-Faw.

There are disputes over the length of the Euphrates and how much of it falls in each of the three co-riparian countries. The most recent figures are from the government of Iraq, which put the length at 2,940 kilometres (km), with 40 per cent in Turkey, 20.5 per cent in Syria and 39.5 per cent in Iraq.

Although more than two thirds of the drainage area lies outside Turkey, 93 per cent of the water in the river originates in Turkey – although some put the percentage at 88 per cent and others at 98 per cent. The drainage area of the Euphrates is widely accepted as 444,000 square kilometres (km^2). However, as with the length of the river flowing through each country, the share of each state in the basin is hotly disputed. Some authorities put the Turkish share at 28 per cent, with Syria at 17 per cent, Iraq 40 per cent and Saudi Arabia 15 per cent. Others apportion the relative shares according to the length of the river in each country.

THE TIGRIS RIVER[3]

Like the Euphrates, the Tigris (1,840 km) also flows through Turkey, Syria and Iraq. In Turkey, the Tigris flows through the south-east for about 400 km, forms the border with Syria for 40 km, and flows downstream to Iraq. As with the Euphrates, there is controversy over the river's length, its drainage area and each country's share of the river. Iraqi government figures put the drainage area at 235,000 km^2, of which 105,750 km^2 (45 per cent) is in Iraq. Figures produced by geographer Hillel put Iraq's share of the basin at 78 per cent, Turkey's share at 20 per cent and Syria's at 2 per cent.[4] The river's flow is characterized by a high annual and seasonal variability. The annual mean flow rate is 520 m^3/s at the border between Turkey and Syria (16.2 billion m^3, or Bm^3, in a year). The lowest flow was 9.6 Bm^3 in 1973, and the highest was 34.3 Bm^3 in 1969. Mean flow in April is 1,433 m^3/s, while the driest month September is 113 m^3/s. Downstream, at Baghdad, the average flow is 1,236 m^3/s.[5]

TURKEY, SYRIA, IRAQ AND DAMS ON BOTH RIVERS[6]

In the case of the Tigris and Euphrates basins, the role that dams have played in exacerbating conflict between the major riparian States – Turkey, Syria and Iraq – is clear. All three countries rely on the waters of the Euphrates and Tigris for their agriculture and future development. Unsurprisingly, the development of engineering projects on the two rivers, notably large dams and irrigation works, has been a source of growing tension between the riparian states. Although outright violence has been avoided, hostilities have mounted each time that a new dam has been built or proposed. On at least three occasions, such hostilities have brought the various parties to the brink of war, with troops being mobilized and threats made to bomb existing dams.

Iraq, the last downstream state on the rivers, was the first to develop dams on the Euphrates, constructing the Hindiya barrage on the Euphrates in 1914 and a second barrage at al-Ramadi in the

1950s.[7] Although both Turkey and Syria began feasibility studies for developing the two rivers in the mid-1950s,[8] neither country undertook construction of any major works until 1966 when Syria started the Tabqa High Dam, later renamed al-Thawrah ('The Revolution'), on the Euphrates and Turkey began construction of the Keban Dam, also on the Euphrates.

Both dams triggered major international disputes. The start of construction on the Keban Dam prompted protests from Syria to Turkey, whilst the completion of the Tabqa Dam led Iraq to threaten military action in 1974 and again in 1975,[9] with both Syria and Iraq mobilizing their troops and moving them to the border.[10] Mediation by the Soviet Union and Saudi Arabia diffused the crisis after Syria agreed to release more water from the dam. Subsequently an agreement was reached between Syria and Iraq whereby Iraq receives 58 per cent of the Euphrates water crossing the Syrian–Turkey border. The agreement has greatly eased tension between the two countries, leading to what Syrian government sources describe as 'an era of cooperation between the two countries over water'.[11]

TURKEY'S GAP PROJECT[12]

Relations between Syria and Iraq on the one hand, and Turkey on the other, have however remained tense, with both Syria and Iraq expressing grave concerns over Turkey's ambitious Southeast Anatolia Project, known as GAP, after its Turkish name 'Guneydogu Anadolu Projesi'. Under the GAP, the Turkish government plans to develop a cluster of 14 dams in the Euphrates basin and eight in the Tigris. Noting the strategic importance of the Tigris and Euphrates, a report by the UK Defence Forum has warned that the GAP project as a whole is:

> [O]ne of the region's most dangerous water time bombs. The dispute has not erupted yet because the project has not yet reached its full potential. By the time of its planned completion in 2010, the vital interests involved give it the potential to become one of the region's most dangerous flashpoints.[13]

Launched in 1977[14] and covering nine provinces with a total area of 74,000 square kilometres, the $32 billion project[15] is the largest development project ever undertaken in Turkey, and one of the largest of its kind in the world.[16] When completed, a total of 90 dams and 60 power plants[17] will have been built on the two river basins, regulating 28 per cent of Turkey's total water potential. In addition to generating 27 billion kilowatt hours of electricity,[18] the dams would be used to irrigate 1.7 million hectares of land in order to grow cash crops and encourage the growth of agro-industries, such as food processing for export.[19] According to Dogan Altinbilek, Director General of DSI, the project 'has top national priority'.[20]

The newly irrigated land would increase the area in Turkey under irrigation by 40 per cent. Based on 1994 figures, the GAP authorities predict that the project will eventually increase vegetable production by 40 per cent, cotton by 300 per cent, barley by 40 per cent and wheat by 100 per cent. Around the Ataturk Dam, the region has been transformed into one of the most important centres of cotton production in Turkey.[21] Overall, it is claimed that the GAP will generate 3.8 million jobs and raise per capita income in the region by 209 per cent.[22]

Numerous government departments are involved in the implementation of GAP, under the aegis of the Southeastern Anatolia Project Regional Development Administration (GAPRDA).

To date, Turkey has invested some $14 billion from its own domestic resources in GAP, with international institutions and the private sector investing a further $3.5 billion.[23] Of the planned water projects, twelve dams and six hydroelectric power plants have already been built – including the giant Ataturk, Karakaya, Keban and Birecik dams. Sixty per cent of the planned hydroelectric plants are running, generating 15 per cent of Turkey's total electricity production. As of December 1999, 11 per cent of the total planned irrigation target had been achieved, with 8 to 10 per cent under construction.

SYRIAN AND IRAQI CONCERNS OVER THE GAP PROJECT[24]

Turkey argues that the GAP project is key to its future economic development. Although both Syria and Iraq are at pains to point out that they respect Turkey's right to develop, both countries fear that the GAP project will result in serious downstream impacts, including dramatically reduced flow and increased levels of pollution. Both countries also fear that Turkey is using the GAP to establish control over the waters of the Tigris and Euphrates as part of a wider policy of establishing regional hegemony.

Reduction in water flow[25]

Much of the water stored in GAP dams is intended for irrigation. According to the GAP administration, the dams that form part of the GAP project would be used to irrigate a total of 1.7 million hectares of land.[26]

As regard the Tigris, according to Syrian sources,[27] if fully completed, GAP projects on the Tigris are scheduled to irrigate a total of 601,824 hectares. On the basis of the figures published by the GAP authorities, Iraq calculates that the Tigris irrigation projects will consume 5.8 Bm^3 [28] and reduce the flow of the Tigris as it passes the border into Syria at Cizre by 66 per cent[29] – from an annual 16.72 Bm^3 [30] to 5.58 Bm^3. Allowing for the water received by the Tigris from tributaries in Syria, Iraq estimates that it would receive 47 per cent less water than at present. According to the Iraqi authorities:

> Such a big shortage in the Tigris River resources will have grave repercussions for Iraq. The majority of Iraq's population depends on the Tigris to meet their drinking water needs, agricultural requirements and others. Agriculture has been practiced for thousands of years along the said river and technical studies have shown that a decrease of 1 Bm^3 in the river's resources will result in the non-use of arable lands estimated at 62,500 hectares (ha). Since the current river's resources suggest a drop of 11.14 Bm^3, the total agricultural area which will be deprived of water in Iraq will reach 696,000 ha. The non-use of such areas will have severe consequences for the entire agricultural production and the water supply for existing farms, as well as other social and economic repercussions on farmers deprived of agricultural requirements, let alone the problem of desertification which will be exacerbated as a result of the above mentioned reduction of arable lands.[31]

Iraq also predicts that the reduced flow 'will be reflected badly on power generation' from the Saddam and Samara dams.[32] 'It is expected that power production in Saddam Dam will drop at a rate close to that of water reduction in the discharges coming to the dam: that is to say, that reduction of power generation in Saddam Dam will drop by approximately 53 per cent.'[33]

Syria, which has a similar dependency on the downstream flow of the Euphrates, forecasts similar problems arising from reduced flow of that river. Before the construction of the Keban Dam in 1966, Turkey used just 3 per cent of the waters of the Euphrates for irrigation.[34] If GAP is completed, the total irrigated area for the Euphrates basin in Turkey will increase to 1,628,203 hectares,[35] requiring 9–16.9 Bm^3 of water a year. Syrian officials estimate that the downstream flow of the Euphrates as it crosses the Syrian border will be reduced by 30–60 per cent.[36] In effect, 'Turkey is planning to use completely half of the Euphrates yield, leaving Syria and Iraq the other half. Moreover, 11 per cent of this half will be of lower quality water since it is return irrigation water from Turkey.'[37]

Increased water pollution[38]

The original planning for the GAP project appears to have paid little attention to the problem of return flows from irrigation schemes. Both Syria and Iraq fear that the result will be increased levels of salinity in the waters of the Tigris and Euphrates, a problem which will be compounded by pesticide and fertilizer run-off and by increased sewage discharges from the new urban centres that GAP is seeking to stimulate. As Syrian officials told the KHRP Fact-Finding Mission (see final section of this chapter for details of the Mission):

> Deterioration of water quality results in a series of problems with negative impacts on human health and environment. The use of contaminated water in irrigation results in the transmission of contaminants to the irrigated plants and consequently to humans, as well as increasing soil salinity, reducing productivity and converting areas of agricultural land into barren land. The deterioration of water quality definitely reduces the uses to which the water can be put, even if it does not render the water completely unusable for human or agricultural consumption. This can create a shortage in water supply, converting the quality problem into a quantity problem.[39]

Estimates vary, but one independent study has predicted that insecticide levels in the Syrian portion of the Euphrates and its tributaries could increase by 35 per cent.[40] Technical studies conducted by Iraq have also forecast a doubling of salinity levels in the Tigris as a result of upstream irrigation in Turkey.[41] Iraq also believes that existing dam projects on the Tigris and Euphrates will affect about 1.3 million hectares of agricultural land – some 40 per cent of the agricultural land available – as a result of declining water quality.[42]

Turkish ambition to control its neighbours[43]

There are also fears that the dams that Turkey has built – or intends to build – will enable Turkey to exercise control over its downstream neighbours. Such fears are not without foundation. Over the years, Turkey has made a number of statements that leave little room for doubting its 'first come, first served' approach to the waters of the Tigris and Euphrates. In 1992, for example, Turkey's Prime Minister Suleyman Demirel stated: 'Neither Syria nor Iraq can lay claim to Turkey's rivers any more than Ankara could claim their oil. This is a matter of sovereignty. We have a right to do anything we like. The water resources are Turkey's; the oil resources are theirs. We don't say we share their oil resources, and they cannot share our water resources.'[44] In recent years Turkey's tone has, in the words of *The Economist*, 'softened somewhat from outright belligerence to studied imprecision'.[45] Nonetheless, despite the talk of collaboration over the use of the Tigris and Euphrates, the language is still uncompromising. Commenting on a series of dams that Turkey intends to build on the Uphort river, Turkey's Deputy Prime Minister Mesut Yilmaz told the Arab daily newspaper *Asharq Al-Awsat* in February 2001:

> We have completed works in almost 50 per cent of the infrastructure and we are in the meantime working on the final stages, and we will extend the invitation to Syria to accept the inevitability of this project and to join negotiations on a rational use of waters. We are ready to deal fairly and generously, but the division of waters will not be equal, as the Euphrates, like any other Turkish river, should be basically used for serving the interests of the Turkish people.[46]

Turkey's aggressive water politics were illustrated most dramatically in 1990, when Turkey blocked the flow of the Euphrates for 9 days whilst filling the reservoir of the Ataturk Dam.[47] Both Syria and Iraq accused Turkey of failing to inform them of the cut-off, prompting Iraq to threaten to bomb all the Euphrates dams.[48] Turkey's Ministry of Foreign Affairs rebutted such claims, arguing that its co-riparians had 'been informed in a timely way that river flow would be interrupted for a period of one month, due to technical necessity',[49] and that, prior to impoundment, more water than usual was released downstream, in order to allow Syria and Iraq to store sufficient waters to carry them through the impoundment period.[50] Turkey also argued that the *average* flow downstream never fell below 500 m³/s – the minimum agreed under a 1987 Protocol signed between Turkey and Syria.[51] This is disputed by both Syria and Iraq, which point out that the decision to release 'extra' water downstream prior to impoundment was taken unilaterally by Turkey and without sufficient notice. Syria also notes that whilst the average monthly discharge at Jarablus on the Turkish–Syrian border for the year 1989–90 may not have fallen far below the agreed 500 m³/s,[52] the monthly discharge in January and February 1990 was far lower – 321 m³/s and 320 m³/s respectively. The Mission reviewed the discharge data from the measuring station at Jarablus and found the Syrian case persuasive.

The Ataturk incident serves as a constant reminder to Syria and Iraq of the potential hold which the GAP project, even uncompleted, gives Turkey over its downstream neighbours. Turkey's three major dams on the Euphrates – Keban, Karakaya and Ataturk – have a storage capacity (some 90–100 Bm³ of water) which greatly exceeds the *entire* annual flow of both the Tigris and Euphrates put together.[53] Should Turkey decide to cut off downstream flow completely, it would therefore have the means to do so for a considerable period of time. Inevitably, questions have been raised as to why Turkey should have built in such huge surplus storage capacity.

Even if an agreement is reached on water sharing, assurances that downstream flow rates will be maintained will ultimately depend on Turkey's political ambitions in the region. Turkey's membership of NATO, its close relations with the US and its acceptance for application for membership of the EU all place it in a strong bargaining position vis-à-vis its downstream neighbours, particularly Iraq, which has been weakened economically and militarily by a decade of sanctions. Indeed, officials in both Iraq and Syria expressed the view that Turkey had taken advantage of the sanctions against Iraq – and its pariah status internationally – to push ahead with its GAP projects on the Tigris, on the assumption that opposition from Iraq (the major downstream co-riparian, since the Tigris only flows through Syria for 40 kilometres) would be either ignored or muted. Whilst consideration of UN policy towards Iraq is outside of the Mission's remit, the Mission was gravely concerned by the destabilizing effects of sanctions on regional power relations, in addition to their evident impact on the Iraqi people and in particular poorer sections of Iraqi society.[54] The Mission recalls the finding of the World Commission on Dams that water conflict is intimately connected to imbalances of power amongst riparian states, and is of the firm view that continued sanctions are potentially stoking the fires of future conflict in the region. The Mission was also disturbed to learn of the wide range of agricultural equipment and equipment relating to water engineering projects that had been denied to Iraq by the UN Sanctions Committee.[55] The denial of such equipment can only result in lower food production and, in the case of irrigation pumps, increased salinization and environmental damage. The Mission considers this unacceptable.

GAP-RELATED TENSION[56]

The first dam to be built under GAP was the Karakaya Dam (constructed 1976–87) on the Euphrates. Other dams have quickly followed – the Ataturk Dam (1983–92), the Karkamis Dam (1996–99) and most recently the Birecik Dam (1993–2000). GAP projects on the Tigris include the Dicle Dam (1986–97) and the Batman Dam (1986–98).[57]

As noted above, tensions came to a head in 1990 when the Turkish authorities effectively halted the flow of the Euphrates altogether in order to fill the Ataturk Dam. Further protests by Syria and Iraq were lodged with Turkey in 1993, prior to the construction of the Birecik Dam on the Euphrates.[58] The same year, with many GAP dams at a low level due to drought, Turkey 'chose to turn off the tap during the Muslim Feast of the Sacrifice in June, reducing the flow from 500 cubic metres per second to 170'[59] in contravention of its agreement under the 1987 Protocol with Syria.

In 1999 and 2000, the two downstream states also protested that they had not been consulted on the proposed construction of the Ilisu Dam on the Tigris, in contravention of international law and bilateral agreements.[60] The Turkish authorities denied the charge, arguing that it had informed Syria and Iraq of its plans with regard to every GAP project.[61]

The Turkish government also claimed that, contrary to Syrian and Iraqi fears, Ilisu would not adversely affect downstream flow. Independent analysis of the data presented in the Environmental Impact Assessment Report (EIAR) for the project, however, flatly contradicts the Turkish government's claim.[62] The analysis found that the construction and operation of the Ilisu Dam by itself would significantly affect the hydrology of the Tigris River. It would alter the seasonal flow pattern by capturing all except large flood flows in the spring and releasing them in the autumn, and would create large daily flow fluctuations whose influence would be felt more than 65 km downstream at the Syrian border. In addition, the operation of the Ilisu Dam in combination with diversions from the future downstream irrigation project at Cizre on the Syrian border would probably significantly reduce summer flows in Syria and Iraq below historic levels. It is likely that a significant portion of the recommended minimum flow release from Ilisu of 60 m³/s during dry years would be diverted. It is even possible that, with full implementation of the Ilisu/Cizre projects, during drought periods *all* the summer flow could be diverted before it crossed the border.

In 2000 tensions again mounted when Turkey once more announced that it would be unable to meet the agreed downstream flow of 500 m³/s to Syria, as a result of drought.

ATTEMPTS TO NEGOTIATE[63]

Although Syria and Iraq have both sought to negotiate a tripartite agreement on the sharing of the Euphrates and Tigris waters, Turkey has refused to come to the table,[64] insisting on linking any negotiation to other issues such as Syria's alleged support during the 1980s for the Kurdistan Workers Party (PKK), and more recently the ongoing border dispute over Iskenderun.[65]

Syria and Iraq assert that their desire to reach a tripartite agreement on future use of the rivers is based both on hard evidence of the severe damage that has already been done by Turkey's dam building project, and on the prospect of further severe damage should the dam project be completed without reaching any collective agreement on Turkey's use of the water. Syria's Deputy Foreign Minister, Mr Waleed Mu'allim, told the Mission:

> Water is life. Many analysts believe disputes over water will be a major cause of military conflict in the region. We want water to be a source of cooperation. We want to resolve this peacefully and in accordance with international law. But if the GAP project goes ahead as planned and without an agreement, within five years more than 7 million Syrians would suffer from salt water pollution and damage to agriculture and drinking water. We are doing our best to attract Turkey to the table to negotiate and to prevent military conflict.[66]

Turkey insists that it has consulted fully with its downstream neighbours on its proposed dams and that it is ensuring adequate

downstream flow of good quality water. Although a number of Iraq–
Turkey and Turkey–Syria agreements have been negotiated, Turkey
has not, in the view of the Syrian government, respected them.[67]
In 1987, for example, Turkey agreed to ensure a minimum average
monthly flow of the Euphrates across the border to Syria of 500 cubic
m^3/s over a full year. However, the flow often falls below that level in
the summer months. In July 1999 official Turkish figures put the flow
at 343 m^3/s and on one occasion the flow was stopped entirely.

Iraq also questions the good faith of the Turkish government.

> The insistence of Turkey in continuing the implementation of the
> Southeast Anatolia Project (GAP), in spite of the repeated objections
> of Iraq and Syria, constitutes a flagrant violation of the principles
> and rules of international law . . . Turkey ignores all legal rules that
> bind it to coordinate and consult with Iraq. Meanwhile, Turkey
> tries to legalise this deliberate neglect through interpreting those
> rules in such a manner that corresponds with its own interests,
> regardless of the interests of the other littoral states.[68]

Iraq and Syria thus continue to call on the Arab League to unite
against Turkey over the GAP. Indeed, the League has passed a number
of resolutions expressing concern over the building of dams on the
Tigris and Euphrates.[69]

FACT-FINDING MISSION[70]

The London-based Kurdish Human Rights Project has conducted a
number of Fact-Finding Missions to the region regarding the Ilisu
Dam, often in association with other NGOs.[71] A Fact-Finding Mission
undertaken by the Kurdish Human Rights Project and The Corner
House in July 2002 concluded that GAP dams have already caused a
significant change in the flow regime of the Euphrates and to a lesser
extent the Tigris. The mission supported the view expressed by Syrian
officials that, whilst water quality in Syria has yet to be seriously
affected by GAP dams, the full implementation of GAP would have
major adverse consequences. The Mission also found that the reduced
flow of the Euphrates has already caused increased salinity in the
lower reaches of the river, seriously affecting agriculture.

The Mission also commented that the system of consultations
between Syria and Iraq regarding the two rivers was well established
and operated well. The agreement to share the waters of the Euphrates

58–42 per cent works smoothly, even during times when political relations are difficult. In comparison, the Mission could not say the same regarding consultation between Turkey and its co-riparians. The Mission found Turkey's claim that its downstream co-riparians had been consulted on GAP projects within the tripartite technical committees that met between 1972 and 1991 to be without substance.

7
International Relations

'Syria still allows its territory and parts of Lebanon to be used by terrorists who seek to destroy every chance of peace in the region. You have passed, and we are applying, the Syrian Accountability Act. And we expect the Syrian government to end all support for terror and open the door to freedom.'

George W. Bush, President, United States of America[1]

International relations with Syria range from the positive relations with Russia and Arab League states to the more awkward dealings with the US and Europe. Traditional Cold War allies such as Russia have supported Syria, to the extent that Russia forgave several billion dollars of Syria's debt during Bashar al-Asad's January 2005 visit to Moscow. During the same visit, Syrian–Russian talks are believed to have resulted in several cooperation agreements, re-strengthening ties between the two countries.

Overall, Syria's relations with the West have been less positive although until recently, Europe and the US took different stances in their relationship with Syria. Whilst US relations with Syria have been strained for many years over allegations of Syrian support for terrorism, since 11 September 2001 the US has adopted an increasingly accusatory tone towards Syria, alleging Syrian involvement in weapons of mass destruction and terrorism and adding Syria to its 'Axis of Evil'. In contrast, Europe has sought a more constructive approach to Syria, negotiating an Association Agreement and using closer relations as a means to address issues such as human rights and weapons of mass destruction.

Following the 2003 Iraq War American attention has shifted towards Syria, Iran and North Korea, countries which the US views as posing the main threat in its 'War on Terror'. Although Iran appeared to be bearing the brunt of US attention, the assassination of former Lebanese Prime Minister Rafik Hariri in February 2005 caused that attention to be deflected onto Syria. As protests against the killing increased, many of Syria's traditional allies turned against it, encouraging Syria to comply with UN Resolution 1559 and withdraw from Lebanon. This resulted in Syria's agreement to redeploy its troops in the Lebanon, moving them back to the Syrian border.

SYRIA AND EUROPE

The Euro-Mediterranean Partnership

In November 1995, a conference held in Barcelona marked the beginning of the Euro-Mediterranean Partnership (Barcelona Process). The Euro-Mediterranean Conference of Ministers of Foreign Affairs aimed to lay out a framework of political, economic and social relations between the European Union Member States and Partner States of the Southern Mediterranean. This Euro-Mediterranean Partnership consists of 35 members, including the now 25 EU Member States and the 10 Mediterranean Partners: Algeria, Egypt, Israel, Jordan, Lebanon, Morocco, Palestinian Authority, Syria, Tunisia and Turkey.[2] May 2004 saw two of the Mediterranean Partners – Cyprus and Malta – enter the European Union.

The Barcelona Process marks the creation of a new regional relationship, with three main objectives:

- Political and Security Chapter: The demarcation of a common area of peace and stability through the reinforcement of political and security dialogue.
- Economic and Financial Chapter: The formation of an economic and financial partnership and the gradual creation of a free trade area.
- Social, Cultural and Human Chapter: The establishment of friendly relations between peoples through a social, cultural and human partnership aimed at encouraging understanding between cultures and exchanges between civil societies.

To achieve these objectives, the Partnership encompasses two main spheres of activity. The EU carries out bilateral activities with each country, including the negotiation of Association Agreements with individual Mediterranean Partners. These Agreements contain general principles regarding the relationship but also reflect the different characteristics in the relationship between the EU and each Mediterranean Partner. The EU also carries out multilateral activities, dealing with problems common to most of its Mediterranean partners.

These activities receive technical and financial support from the MEDA programme, which committed €3,435 million between 1995 and 1999 to support cooperation programmes and other projects. A further €5,350 million has been set aside for activities between 2000 and 2006. Further support has come from the European Investment Bank, which provided €4,808 million between 1995 and 1999 and has allocated a further €6,400 million up to 2006. These financial resources are subject to programming. For this, Strategy Papers are drawn up covering the period 2000 to 2006 at a national and regional level. Three-year national indicative programmes (NIPs) are drawn up for the bilateral activities, with a regional indicative programme covering the multilateral activities.

Based on its Country Strategy Paper for Syria, the main challenges facing Syria over the medium term are diminishing oil reserves, rapid population growth, environmental degradation and the military and political conflict with Israel. The EU believes it can most effectively assist Syria by focusing on five key sectors: institution-building, industrial modernization, human resources development, trade enhancement, and human rights/civil society.[3]

On 19 October 2004, the European Commission and Syria announced an end to negotiations for an EU-Syria Association Agreement. With the other Mediterranean partners having already concluded their Association Agreements, this Agreement represented the completion of a network with all participants in the Barcelona Process.[4]

The EU–Syria Association Agreement

Although negotiations on the EU–Syria Association Agreement began in 1998, they achieved little progress. It was not until 2001, when Bashar al-Asad reorganized the government and placed reform-minded ministers into ministries, that progress was made. This progress and associated priority on reform was continued by the new government under Prime Minister Al-'Utari, who took over in September 2003. By 9 December 2003, all technical negotiations relating to the Agreement had been concluded and other than being politically approved by both parties, the Agreement was ready for signature.[5]

On 19 October 2004, the European Commission and Syria marked the formal end to negotiations for the Association Agreement. With the other Mediterranean partners having already concluded their Association Agreements, this Agreement represented the completion of a network with all participants in the Barcelona Process.[6] The

Agreement covers three main areas of politics, economics and social and cultural matters.

Politics

The Agreement creates a framework to enable regular political dialogue on international issues of common interest. The framework covers topics including the respect for democratic principles and fundamental human rights, anti-terrorism and cooperation on working against the creation of weapons of mass destruction.

Economics

The Agreement foresees the creation of a free trade area between the EU and Mediterranean Partners by 2010 and covers a variety of economic issues to enable future free trade between the EU and Syria. These issues include rules for trade in goods and services, rules of public procurement and cooperation in areas such as customs, tourism and the environment.

Social and cultural matters

The Agreement also foresees cooperation in an array of areas such as education, culture, racism and xenophobia, the fight against crime, the rule of law, legal and judicial cooperation and the movement of persons.

Weapons of mass destruction

On 12 December 2003, the European Council adopted a European Security Strategy, 'A Secure Europe in a Better World'. One of the major threats identified over the next ten years was the proliferation of weapons of mass destruction (WMD). The Strategy adopted by the European Council provides a clear guide on action to be taken in the fight against the proliferation of WMD.[7]

In a six-monthly Progress Report dated December 2004, it was reported that following negotiations with Syria, the Association Agreement initialled on 19 October 2004 contained a WMD clause under which Syria agreed to cooperate with the EU to counter the proliferation of weapons of mass destruction and their means of delivery.[8] The EU has therefore taken a more positive approach toward dealing with allegations of Syrian WMD by forming a partnership with Syria to work together on the issue, instead of accusing Syria and demanding results.

Human rights

Despite negotiating with Syria to conclude the Association Agreement, the European Union has been prominent in criticizing Syria over domestic human rights abuses.[9] The EU has publicly made clear that it hoped the overall human rights situation in Syria would have developed more positively following Bashar al-Asad's accession to power. Following the Damascus Spring, the EU was vocal in its protests over many of the arrests and convictions of opposition figures and human rights advocates.

More specifically with regard to the Kurdish issue, the EU has criticized Syria over its treatment of the Kurdish population that has never received Syrian citizenship. Despite promising to deal with this issue, the EU institutions have noted that the Syrian government is yet to produce negligible results in this area. The EU has also expressed concerns over the serious human rights abuses that appear to have occurred following the disturbances between Kurds and Arabs in Qamishli and the surrounding regions.

In its 2003 Annual Report on Human Rights, the European Council stated that the human rights situation in Syria had been addressed in an EU statement to the Commission on Human Rights (CHR). Although the EU was said to be 'encouraged' by Syria's decision to release 600 political prisoners and grant licences to individual publications, the report stated that the EU remained concerned about the overall human rights situation in that country:

> There have been reports of widespread use of torture in Syrian prisons and a lack of accountability of the security services. The EU deplored politically motivated arrests and trials of prominent members of civil society and journalists for peacefully exercising their freedom of expression, as well as the sentences against two members of parliament.[10]

In its own Annual Report of 2003 on Human Rights, the European Parliament summarized its own external human rights activities.[11] In the case of Syria, the report referred to hearings that had been held with civil society representatives focusing on political prisoners within Syria, making special reference to the case of Riad Al Turk.

Riad Al Turk, a leading member of the National Democratic Alliance[12] and First Secretary of the Syrian Communist Party, had previously been detained without charge or trial between 1980 and 1998. In September 2001 Al Turk was re-arrested as part of the government crackdown following the Damascus Spring, tried before the Supreme State Security Court and in 2002 was sentenced to two and a half years in prison on charges including 'attempting to change the constitution by illegal means'.[13] Shortly after the hearing, the European Parliament issued a resolution calling for Al Turk's immediate release; Riad Al Turk was later released under a personal presidential amnesty on 16 November 2002.

The European Parliament resolution calling for Riad Al Turk's release also called on the Syrian authorities to, amongst other things: ensure that detainees were well treated and not subjected to torture or other ill-treatment, and ratify the Convention against Torture and Other Cruel, Inhuman or Degrading Treatment or Punishment without reservation and implement its provisions.[14] On 19 August 2004, Syria acceded to the Convention against Torture and Other Cruel, Inhuman or Degrading Treatment or Punishment. However, in accordance with Article 28 of the CAT, Syria declared that it did not recognize the competence of the Committee Against Torture provided for in Article 20 of the CAT.

Under Article 20, if information appears to contain well-founded indications that torture is being systematically practised in the territory of a State Party, the Committee can conduct an inquiry, visit the territory of a State Party or request the State Party to submit observations on the information. In inserting this declaration, Syria has effectively removed the possibility of action being taken against it when human rights organizations or individuals allege that Syria has carried out torture.

Syria also declared that its accession to the Convention Against Torture did not signify recognition of Israel, nor would it entail entry into any dealings with Israel in the context of the provisions of the Convention.

SYRIA AND THE UNITED STATES

US–Syrian relations were severed in 1967 and not restored until the June 1974 Syrian–Israeli disengagement agreement. By the early 1990s, US–Syrian relations were at a high, with Syria cooperating as a member of the multinational coalition forces in the 1990 Gulf War and with the US and Syria working together on the Ta'if Accord to end civil war in Lebanon.

However, the US has long held concerns over Syria, particularly with regard to terrorism. When the US first drew up a list of state sponsors of terrorism in 1979 Syria was on the list and has not yet been removed, making it ineligible for most US aid. US concerns also existed regarding Syrian support for terrorist groups including Lebanese Hezbollah, Palestinian Hamas and Islamic Jihad both in Syria and Lebanon, Syria's continued presence in Lebanon in defiance of the Ta'if Accord and Syrian human rights abuses. Towards the end of the 1990s, these concerns widened to include Syria's pursuit of weapons of mass destruction, causing US–Syrian relations to weaken even further. As US relations have swung between constructive engagement and public condemnation of Syria with corresponding applications of diplomatic and economic pressure, legislation has been periodically introduced to further US aims. Most recently, formal US pressure on Syria was seen in the Syria Accountability and Lebanese Sovereignty Act (SALSA).

Since the removal of Saddam Hussein's Ba'thist regime in Iraq in April 2003, Syria has become increasingly singled out as one of the two pariah states of the Middle East region, the other being Iran. Along with the increased sense of isolation, recent events in early 2005 have increased tensions between Syria on the one hand, and the US and Lebanon on the other.

Iraq

Syria voted in favour of UN Security Council Resolution 1441 in 2002, which recognized Iraq's failure to cooperate with United Nations inspectors and the International Atomic Energy Agency over weapons of mass destruction, and provided for the creation of an enhanced inspection regime. However, Syrian opposition to coalition military action in Iraq in 2003, caused a further deterioration in Syrian–US relations. Syria did later vote for Resolution 1511 which called for greater international involvement in Iraq and addressed the transfer of sovereignty from the US-led coalition. Although the US acknowledged that following the transfer of sovereignty in Iraq on 28 June 2004, Syria pledged to cooperate on border security, repatriation of Iraqi assets and the eventual restoration of formal diplomatic relations, the US continued to display concern that Syria remained 'one of the primary transit points for foreign fighters and weapons entering Iraq'.[15]

Syria is alleged to have taken in fugitives of the former Iraqi regime and also to have encouraged armed fighters to cross from Syria to

Iraq, taking military equipment with them and using this to fight against coalition troops. Perhaps trying to rebut these claims, reports in February 2005 suggest that Syria was instrumental in capturing and handing over to coalition forces Sabawi Ibrahim al-Hasan al-Tikriti, the half-brother of Saddam Hussein. Al-Tikriti was on the US list of most-wanted people in Iraq, as an intelligence chief and former adviser to Saddam.[16]

Again during the buildup to the 2005 Iraq elections, the US claimed that Syria was supporting the insurgents within Iraq and helping both fighters and weapons to enter Iraq, demanding the Syrian government put a stop to this practice.

Weapons of mass destruction

Being designated a state sponsor of terrorism has also laid Syria open to US allegations on weapons of mass destruction. The US has previously alleged that Syria possesses WMD and that some of these weapons may have come from Iraq. At the same time, there is no evidence that Syria has ever used weapons of mass destruction. However, these allegations have served to further sour relations between the countries.

Syrian accountability and Lebanese Sovereignty Act

The original Syria Accountability Act was drawn up in September 2002 by supporters of Lebanese sovereignty within the House of Representatives who urged the US to rethink its appeasement of Syria. However, the Bush administration distanced itself from the bill, which was then revised and presented to the House in April 2003 as the Syria Accountability and Lebanese Sovereignty Act (SALSA or SAA). This Act outlined a sanctions regime for Syria based on allegations that Syria held a secret chemical and biological weapons arsenal, that it was deliberately aiding the resistance to the US-led presence in Iraq and that it continued to occupy Lebanon.

The White House rejected SALSA in early 2003, as the imposition of sanctions on Syria was viewed as limiting the United States' ability to address important issues in both Syria and the surrounding region at a critical juncture in US–Middle Eastern relations. However, in the aftermath of the Iraq War, the rhetoric of the US administration noticeably changed. Syrian cooperation was suddenly viewed as being of less importance and US officials began publicly condemning Syrian support for terrorism and 'occupation' of Lebanon, threatening to exclude it from the Middle East peace process. As of October 2003, the

Bush administration no longer opposed the bill and on 15 October 2003, the House of Representatives voted in favour of imposing economic and diplomatic sanctions on Syria until Syria withdrew from Lebanon and ceased its support for terrorist groups. The House was joined by the Senate on 14 November 2003 in approving the legislation and on 12 December 2003, President Bush signed SALSA.

Under SALSA, the penalties that can be imposed include banning US exports to Syria, reducing diplomatic contact and imposing restrictions on Syrian diplomats, freezing Syrian assets in the US, halting the investment of US business in Syria and prohibiting the use of American airports by Syrian aircraft. These sanctions added to action already taken by Washington, including the disconnection of the Iraqi–Syrian oil pipeline.

Whilst SALSA has been effective in increasing economic and external pressures on Syria, it neither addresses the issue of human rights nor calls the Syrian government to account for its human rights abuses.

Lebanon

During the 1975 civil war which was to last for 15 years, Syrian concerns that the fragmentation of Lebanon from Syria would amount to the establishment of 'another Israel' caused Syria to act as mediator. When diplomacy failed, Syria intervened militarily and by the 1980s was the main external actor in Lebanon, imposing its will over much of the country through the presence of Syrian troops.

The civil war was ended by the 1989 Ta'if Agreement, which permitted the presence of Syrian troops in Lebanon but provided that Syria and Lebanon would at a future date agree a timescale for the redeployment of Syrian troops out of Lebanon. However, by 2004 this had still not happened despite repeated calls for withdrawal from the US and other countries and this continued Syrian presence resulted in the UN Security Council passing a resolution on withdrawal.

UN Security Council Resolution 1559 (2004)

Resolution 1559 was intended to reaffirm the Security Council's call for the strict respect of Lebanese sovereignty, territorial integrity, unity and political independence. It declared support for free and fair presidential elections in Lebanon, conducted according to Lebanese constitutional rules devised without foreign interference or influence and, in that connection, called upon all remaining foreign forces to withdraw from Lebanon. Those voting in favour included the US and France, who had introduced the resolution together due to concerns over the apparent ongoing interference with Lebanese political affairs. The US alleged that the Syrian government had 'imposed its political will on Lebanon and had compelled the Cabinet and Lebanese National Assembly to amend its constitution and abort the electoral process by extending the term of the current President by three years. Clearly, the Lebanese Parliament had been pressured, and even threatened, by Syria and its agents to make them comply.' In contrast, Russia abstained from the vote, concerned that the wrong move might exacerbate the situation in the region and create further instability.[17]

The events of early 2005

Although Syria had come under further pressure to withdraw from Lebanon, the events of February 2005 brought the issue to the fore. On 14 February 2005 a car bomb exploded in Damascus, killing former Prime Minister Rafik al-Hariri. Hariri had long been opposed to the Syrian presence in Lebanon and although Syria denied any involvement in the assassination, international suspicion immediately began to focus on Syria. The most obvious example of this was seen when the United States recalled its ambassador to Syria soon after the attack. This action was intended to express US frustration with Syria's behaviour in Lebanon: although the US acknowledged they did not know who was to blame for the attack, officials argued that Syria's military presence and political role in the country was generally responsible for Lebanon's instability. By removing the ambassador, the US could show its anger at Syrian dominance of the Lebanese military and political system.[18]

During the mourning period, thousands of protestors took to the streets in Lebanon, blaming Bashar al-Asad for Hariri's death and attacking Syrian workers. Opposition leaders including Druze leader Walid Jumblatt implicated Syria in the murder, arguing that as the Syrians were in control of Lebanese security services they bore responsibility for failing to protect Hariri from attack.[19] On the day of Mr Hariri's funeral, tens of thousands of Lebanese lining the route of the funeral procession mourned but also joined in calls for Syrian troops to leave.[20] On the same day, President Bush also called on Syria to adhere to UN Resolution 1559 by removing its troops and enabling free elections.[21]

The increasing pressure against Syria and Syrian-backed components of the Lebanese state then shifted to the Lebanese government, known allies of Bashar al-Asad. Following two weeks of protests during which thousands of Lebanese demonstrated in Beirut's Martyrs Square, the entire pro-Syrian government of Prime Minister Omar Karami unexpectedly resigned on 28 February 2005.[22] In response to the mass resignation, US Secretary of State Condoleezza Rice declared that the US supported Lebanese aspirations for democracy, calling for the withdrawal of Syrian troops from Damascus and publicly declaring support for free and fair elections.[23] Syria's response to the resignations was to describe them as an internal affair.

Despite, or perhaps as a result of the government resignations, pressure on Syria then increased. Even traditional allies failed to provide support to Syria, instead echoing Western calls for Syria to pull troops out of Lebanon. Russia, a long-standing friend of Syria since the Cold War, had previously abstained when Resolution 1559 was adopted by the UN Security Council in 2004. However, in early March 2005 Russia's Foreign Minister stated that the resolution must be implemented and that Syrian troops should withdraw from Lebanon.[24] And when Bashar al-Asad attended crisis talks in Saudi Arabia, Saudi officials allege Saudi Crown Prince Abdullah made clear to al-Asad that Syria must start withdrawing troops or face difficulties in Saudi–Syrian relations. Hariri had previously spent two decades in Saudi Arabia, had close ties with the Saudi royal family and had taken Saudi citizenship.[25]

Under increasing pressure from the US, Europe and Middle East and with the situation in Lebanon making daily headlines around the world, on 5 March 2005 Bashar al-Asad told the Syrian parliament that Syria would start to pull its troops out of Lebanon, although this did not mean the absence of Syria's role in Lebanon.[26] Two days after his announcement, al-Asad met Lebanese President Emile Lahoud to determine troop withdrawal. Whilst the two presidents announced plans for a two-phase withdrawal immediately following the talks, some Syrian troops had already begun to pack up equipment. Under the two-phase plan, Syrian troops would withdraw to the Beqaa Valley in Lebanon by the end of March 2005 and to the border area in accordance with the Ta'if Agreement soon after.[27]

Whilst the announcement of withdrawal was welcomed by Saudi Arabia,[28] the initial US and Canadian response was that the withdrawal plan was a 'half hearted measure' and only complete withdrawal would be acceptable.[29] It remains to be seen whether Syrian troops do fully withdraw from Lebanon or whether some troops remain within Lebanon, antagonizing the US. Only then is the US likely to determine its final reaction to recent events.

Part Three
The Kurds in Syria

INTRODUCTION

In its periodic report to the United Nations Committee on the Elimination of Racial Discrimination of 1998, Syria stated decisively that:

> [W]e wish to point out that there is no so-called Kurdish problem in the Syrian Arab Republic.[1]

The report continues by stating that:

> The Kurds do not constitute a grouping, since they are found throughout the country and form part of the fabric of Syrian society.[2]

The Kurds resident in Syria continue to be described as a migrant population from Turkey and Iraq that has largely assimilated to Syrian Arab culture. In this way, the Syrian state portrays the Kurds as comprising a dispersed ethnic minority in Syria with no historical claim to the land. This portrayal highlights the effect of the Arabization policy that has been implemented both in Syria and other states with Arab populations.

This Arabization policy is intended to force the assimilation of non-Arab groups into Arabic society and culture by following several key tactics. Removing evidence of a non-Arab group's regional history and existence enables a state to deny any historical non-Arab presence in the area and describe such groups as migrants. Dispersing the non-Arab population throughout the state 'dilutes' the group, again removing evidence of a large non-Arab presence but also reducing the ability of members of the group to coordinate and organize. Finally, restricting the group's expression of its cultural identity forces the group to adapt to Arab culture and practices and forget its own heritage. Within Syria, severe restrictions on the flow of information both in and out of the country have prevented the image of the Kurdish population being 'largely assimilated migrants' from being effectively challenged.

Over time, many other Arab states have toned down their Arabist rhetoric as the ideology became seemingly less potent and relevant to domestic and foreign policy requirements. However, Syria continues to depend on Arabist rhetoric for domestic legitimacy, defence against other Arab leaders and influence in the Arab region. Establishing the Kurds as one of many threats to domestic security was in part a reaction to what was perceived to be a real risk of infiltration from foreign states and of domestic instability. As with other threats, it was also partly a means of rallying domestic support around the regime and its Arabist ideology and policy. Therefore, needs of the regime led to the Kurds being defined as an external source of instability and threat, and a sector of society whose identity should be redefined in line with Arab nationalism. Hence, the policy of Arabization with its strategy of, on the one hand, denying the Kurdish national existence in Syria and suppressing expressions of it, and on the other, forcing Kurdish assimilation to the Arab Syrian state and society.

Although the Kurds were deemed to be a threat to the state even earlier than the 1960s, Arabization of Kurdish areas in Syria did not occur until the early 1960s. As a consequence of this policy, large numbers of Kurds have been stripped of Syrian citizenship and described as 'foreign', supporting the Syrian government's claims that the majority of Kurds in Syria are not historically from Syria. Their land has been expropriated and their economic stability threatened. Kurds face daily restrictions on the use of their language and the practice of cultural traditions.

Although the harshest treatment was meted out to the Kurdish population between the 1950s and 1970s, the state's attitude towards the Kurds has barely altered. The maintenance of its power remains the regime's core concern and perceptions of increased external threat have generally worked to entrench the hardliners within the regime, reinforcing Arabist rhetoric and preventing reform and the development of alternative forms of legitimacy that would allow for the incorporation of Kurdish identity. Since the end of the Cold War Syria has been more isolated and vulnerable to external pressures and changes in regional dynamics. Indeed, all evidence suggests that discrimination against the Kurdish population of Syria continues unabated since Bashar al-Asad came to power.

The Arabization policy applied in Syria mirrors the Arabization policy applied in Iraq and the Turkification policy of Turkey. The removal of Kurds from their land and associated demographic change began with the 1962 Hasakeh census in Syria. Since then, both Turkey and Iraq have altered the demographic makeup of Kurdish regions in their own countries, particularly around strategic defensive and economically profitable areas such as the mountainous border areas of Turkey and Kirkuk in Iraq. Although the tactics implemented by the Turkish and Iraqi authorities were more violent and involved more military force, the basic strategy behind this policy has been the same: to alter the demographics of each country and deny the existence of large Kurdish populations.

The Arabization policy targeting the Kurds of Syria, as with the Kurds of Turkey and Iraq, is based on the perception of the Kurdish population as posing a threat to the state due to their collective national and ethnic identity. Under the International Covenant of Civil and Political Rights, such a policy constitutes racial discrimination. Yet, in a report submitted to the International Convention on the Elimination of all Forms of Racial Discrimination, the Syrian Arab Republic states categorically that:

> Syrian society is distinguished from other societies in the world by its tolerance and lack of bigotry. ... The phenomenon of racial discrimination is unknown in our history and totally alien to our society in which any behaviour or act manifesting or implying racism is regarded as highly reprehensible. Accordingly, our people are engaged in a relentless battle against the manifestations of racism that characterize Israeli ideology.[3]

The changes effected in formerly Kurdish areas have resulted from many different actions by the Syrian state. Part Three of this book discusses in more detail the various ways in which the Kurdish identity, social, political representation and economic well-being has been deliberately eroded by the regime.

8
The Civil Rights of Kurds in Syria

'All rights should be secured to all individuals within a state's territory without any distinction on grounds of race, sex, national or social origin, birth or other status and without any discrimination between men and women' As provided by Article 2 of the Universal Declaration of Human Rights, Article 2 of the Arab Charter on Human Rights and Article 2 of the International Covenant on Civil and Political Rights

The 1962 census in al-Hasakeh province resulted in between 120,000 and 150,000 Kurds losing their Syrian citizenship. Proving Syrian citizenship required one or all of three documents to be shown on the day of the census but, as discussed previously in Part Two of this book, many Kurds were either unable to provide the requisite documents or unwilling, having not been told the purpose of the census.

Consequently, despite the census having been intended to differentiate between those with a right to Syrian nationality and those with no such right, many of the Kurds stripped of their nationality were in fact entitled to be described as Syrian citizens. Instead, they were demoted to *ajanib* (foreign) or *maktoumeen* (unregistered) and underwent a corresponding reduction in their rights.

As mentioned above, at the time of the census between 120,000 and 150,000 Kurds became stateless in the eyes of the Syrian government. By 1995, the Syrian government estimated there were also around 75,000 maktoumeen 'unregistered' Kurds; although the government failed to provide a figure for the number of maktoumeen children. And in 1996, Human Rights Watch estimated that the stateless Kurds then numbered around 200,000.[1]

The treatment accorded to the ajanib and maktoumeen Kurds is a clear violation of both customary international law and the Arab Charter of Human Rights as adopted by the Council of the League of Arab States, of which Syria is a member.

THE RIGHT TO NATIONALITY

Under Article 15 of the Universal Declaration of Human Rights (hereafter 'UDHR'), everyone has the right to nationality. Article 15 further provides, as does Article 24 of the Arab Charter of Human Rights (hereafter 'ACHR'), that no citizen shall be arbitrarily denied of his original nationality. The events of 1962 saw a complete disregard by the Syrian state for the right to nationality, as enshrined in these provisions.

Following the 1962 census in al-Hasakeh province, around 120,000 to 150,000 Kurds who had lived in Syria their entire lives were stripped of their citizenship and classified as foreign or stateless, due to their inability to provide requisite paperwork on the day of the census.

The affected Kurds were divided into two groups: *ajanib* (foreigner) Kurds and *maktoumeen* (unregistered) Kurds. Although the purpose of the census was supposedly to weed out Kurds who had come to Syria after 1945, the arbitrary granting and removal of citizenship status of many Kurds did not support this argument.

Within families, illogical distinctions were made by the authorities. Fathers lost the citizenship that their children managed to retain; brothers were classed as a mixture of ajanib and maktoumeen. Entire families lost their citizenship over night. Human Rights Watch provided many examples, including four Kurdish couples, who were all born in Syria prior to 1935: every couple lost Syrian citizenship and their 25 children became registered as ajanib.[2] At the same time Kurds who, by Syrian government definitions should have been ineligible for citizenship, succeeded in bribing officials to ensure Syrian nationality.[3]

Even Kurdish men who had served in the Syrian army during their national service were at risk; some discovered they no longer held Syrian citizenship whilst undertaking military service. On one occasion, the authorities confiscated documents proving national service had been carried out by a Kurdish man who had been stripped of citizenship, preventing him from regaining his nationality.[4] Other Kurdish men who had been classed as ajanib or maktoumeen have since received conscription documents to undertake national service in the Syrian armed forces. Under Syrian laws, Syrian national service is compulsory for all Syrian nationals over the age of 19.[5]

Whilst some Kurds managed to regain their citizenship through tax records that had been imposed on Syrians during the Ottoman Turkish colonization, Syrian lawyers allege that these records were quickly sealed by the government and thereafter could not be used.[6]

Human Rights Watch is also aware of Kurds who were stripped of citizenship even after the original census, including Kurds who have lost their citizenship whilst undergoing military service and others who graduated from university, were then stripped of their nationality and despite documentation to provide nationality, cannot regain their Syrian citizenship.[7]

The most obvious effect of the denial of nationality can be seen in the identity papers available to ajanib and maktoumeen Kurds. Syrian citizens are registered on the population registers and have an official identity card, which is used in many aspects of daily life. Ajanib Kurds are registered on the foreigners' registry but are not entitled to an official identity card; instead they are given a red identity card which proclaims they are ajanib.[8] Maktoumeen Kurds are not entered onto the official Syrian population register, nor are they permitted any form of identity card. The most that maktoumeen Kurds can obtain is a letter from the village *Mukhtar* (head of the village) attesting to knowing them; but even this basic document is difficult to obtain. This denial of nationality and identity papers has many knock-on effects for the stateless Kurds, as will be discussed in this chapter.

Recent decrees have made it even more difficult to obtain these documents. For example, in October 1999 the mayor of al-Hasakeh province passed a memorandum forbidding the issuance of documents to maktoumeen. Although not fully implanted, decisions such as these have made life difficult for maktoumeen Kurds.[9]

This treatment of Kurds is also in direct contravention of Syrian law. Under Article 2 of Syrian Citizenship Acquisition Law No.276 (1969), nationality is given according to decree No.67 (1961), which states

Nationality of the Syrian Arab Republic is given to those who had Syrian nationality on 21st February 1958.
Nationality of the Syrian Arab Republic is given to those who had the nationality of the United Arab Republic.

Furthermore, the Citizenship Acquisition Law states that it is possible to give foreigners nationality.[10] To qualify, foreign nationals must be over 18, have lived in Syria for five years, be able to work and not suffer from a disease, have a good reputation, possess skills that will benefit the state and be able to read and write Arabic. But because ajanib and maktoumeen Kurds have never held any other nationality, they are excluded from benefiting through this law.

It is overall far easier to acquire Syrian citizenship as a foreign national or child of a foreign national resident in Syria than it is for an ajanib and maktoumeen Kurd who was born and has lived in Syria throughout their life.

As both ajanib *and* maktoumeen Kurds were allocated this status in 1962 and have remained in Syria to this day, they more than qualify under the five years residence requirement, yet the Syrian government has still failed to award them nationality.

Because they do not officially exist, when maktoumeen Kurds die they are not even issued a death certificate.

A CHILD'S RIGHT TO NATIONALITY

Article 7 of the Convention on the Rights of the Child (hereafter 'CRC') and Article 24 of the International Covenant on Civil and Political Rights (hereafter 'ICCPR') provide that every child should be registered after birth and has the right to acquire a nationality.

According to Syrian laws, a child is deemed to be a Syrian Arab under Syrian nationality laws if they were born in Syria to a father with Syrian nationality, born in Syria to parents who were unknown or stateless, or born in Syria to parents who were aliens and whose nationality the child could not acquire.[11] In reality, the denial of nationality to many Kurdish children flouts both Syrian and international law.

Ajanib Kurds are unable to obtain travel documents thus their children are born on Syrian territory. However, although they are entered onto the foreigners' registry and receive a red identity card, ajanib children do not acquire Syrian nationality. Even after spending several years in Syria, ajanib children still remain 'foreign'.

As explained above, maktoumeen Kurds are not registered in the Syrian population registers following their birth; nor do they receive any official identity documents. Kurdish children are classed as maktoumeen in the following situations: firstly, if the child's father is an ajanib Kurd, and the child's mother is a Syrian citizen; secondly, if one of the child's parents is maktoumeen; and thirdly, if the child is born to two maktoumeen Kurds.

These maktoumeen children are in an impossible position. Having never possessed Syrian citizenship, unlike their parents they have not been stripped of their citizenship. At the same time, they were clearly born on Syrian soil and have never left Syria. However, Syrian laws do not appear to apply to them and maktoumeen children are never able to obtain citizenship.

The inevitable population growth has meant that the maktoumeen population is today far larger than the 75,000 estimated to exist in 1995 by the Syrian government.[12] Human Rights Watch provides a good example of the exponential growth of the maktoumeen population, by comparing the situation of three brothers, all of whom are ajanib Kurds. One married a Syrian citizen, one an ajanib Kurd and one a maktoumeen Kurd; of the 26 children born to their families, six are ajanib and the remaining 21 maktoumeen.[13]

In 1996, a report issued to the UN Committee on the Rights of the Child saw the Syrian government state that all children in Syria were treated in a non-discriminatory fashion:[14]

The law protects Syrian and all other children residing in the territory of the state, regardless of race, origin, religion or nationality and without any discrimination between them. No case of discrimination in regard to this protection has ever been reported in Syria.

Syrian children enjoy the same rights without discriminatory treatment on grounds such as race, origin, language or religion. They are treated equally at school and in the various institutions concerned with the welfare and protection of children. They all benefit from the same rights, privileges and services provided by the State.[15]

In spite of this claim, denied of their right to nationality and identity cards in a country where identity cards are required for many aspects of daily life, maktoumeen children are unable to obtain many of the rights listed by the Syrian government. When pressed by Human Rights Watch, the Syrian government failed to provide any explanation as to why these children are unable to obtain an identity card.[16]

Article 7 of the CRC requires states to ensure implementation of a child's right to nationality *particularly* where the child would otherwise be stateless. Syria fails altogether in this regard.

THE RIGHT TO FAMILY LIFE

Article 16 of the UDHR and Article 23 of the ICCPR state that men and women of marriageable age have the right to marry and found a family. Article 15 of the UDHR, Article 23 of the ICCPR and Article

38 of the ACHR further provide that the family is the natural and fundamental group unit of society and as such is entitled to protection by both society and the state.

Syrian women cannot marry ajanib Kurds; if they try to marry a Syrian-born foreigner the marriage is not legally recognized. Any land or property can only be registered in the name of the woman and upon her death, if she has no family, the property will transfer to the state. Neither her husband nor children will be entitled to the property.

Although it is reportedly possible to appeal for recognition of the marriage, a decision in their favour will not affect the official registers which will still recognize neither the marriage nor any children.[17] The Syrian government defends this policy on the grounds that without it, Syrian women would lose their citizenship status. The government has also said that

> in the case that a Syrian female should have the audacity to marry any foreigner, whether he is a foreigner of Hasakeh or elsewhere, that marriage is considered illegal. As a result, neither it nor the children that ensue will be registered in the civil registers.[18]

Syrian practices consequently discriminate against both non-citizen Kurdish males and Syrian women and prevent numerous Kurdish children from being part of a legally recognized family.

FREEDOM OF MOVEMENT

The right to freedom of movement and residence within the borders of each state is guaranteed under Article 13 of the UDHR, Article 12 of the ICCPR and Articles 20 to 22 of the ACHR. Furthermore, everyone should have the right to leave any country including his own, and to return to his country.

The red identity card held by ajanib Kurds is not valid for external travel and, registered only on the foreigner's registry, ajanib Kurds are unable to obtain passports.[19] Unable to claim any nationality other than Syrian, these ajanib Kurds thus cannot obtain any internationally recognized travel documents and consequently cannot leave Syria other than to relocate; although they would then be unable to re-enter Syria.

Maktoumeen Kurds share the fate of ajanib Kurds in that they also cannot travel abroad and re-enter Syria. Travelling internally is also more difficult for maktoumeen; if they are unable to obtain a letter from the village *mukhtar*, they cannot even undertake inter-state travel.

Whilst internal travel is possible for ajanib and maktoumeen Kurds who have obtained a letter from the *mukhtar*, in practice such travel is difficult and tedious. If ajanib or maktoumeen Kurds wish to stay in a hotel overnight, they must obtain permission from the local security forces. As permission is frequently not granted, this restriction drastically impedes the ability of ajanib and maktoumeen Kurds to travel within Syria either for personal reasons or to try and find employment.

THE RIGHT TO PRIVATE PROPERTY

Under Article 17 of the UDHR and Article 25 of the ACHR, every citizen has the right to own private property and shall not be arbitrarily deprived of his property.

Ajanib and maktoumeen Kurds cannot own land, housing or businesses.[20] As a result, when such Kurds die, their ajanib or maktoumeen children cannot inherit their land or other property.

A suburb in Damascus, known as Zor Ava ('built by force'), was built by Kurds working in Damascus who are unable to buy or rent property. Because the suburb was built without permission from the authorities, it could be destroyed at any time.

THE RIGHT TO EDUCATION

Under Article 26 of the UDHR and Article 28 of the CRC, everyone has the right to education which should be free in the elementary and fundamental stages. Elementary education is compulsory, higher education shall be equally accessible to all on the basis of merit and technical and professional education should be made generally available. Article 34 of the ACHR also states that every citizen has a right to education, that primary education shall be compulsory and both secondary and university education shall be made easily accessible to all.

The Syrian Constitution states that it aims to achieve universal education. In spite of this, the ongoing denial of education to ajanib and maktoumeen Kurds contravenes the stipulations of these most basic laws.

The Syrian education system requires nine initial years of study, after which children sit an examination. Upon obtaining a diploma showing that they have passed this examination, children may then study grades ten to twelve and from there move on to higher education.

Ajanib Kurds are able to obtain a diploma and sometimes can study through to university, should they so wish and be able to afford. However, they face difficulties in qualifying and will not be able to obtain state employment. In addition, certain schools, such as military schools, schools of journalism and of medicine, deny access to these Kurds.[21] Even if a stateless Kurd obtains a secondary or higher education, their certificates are not recognized by the Ministry of Education and they have no transferable value for obtaining employment. Ajanib Kurds consequently struggle to obtain jobs reflecting their knowledge and experience.

The Syrian government informed Human Rights Watch in 1996 that maktoumeen are accepted for admission to all schools.[22] To attend elementary school, parents of maktoumeen children must first obtain a letter attesting to the child's maktoumeen status and then obtain permission from the internal Syrian security forces.[23] In obtaining permission, many parents suffer harassment and intimidation from the security forces.[24]

The Human Rights Watch report on Syria and the Kurds of 1996 recounts a Kurdish man's complaints with the procedure endured to simply register his child for first grade:

> One man pointed to his young daughter and said: 'it took me twenty-nine days, going to the police area director, to the security apparatus, to the birth registration office, just to register her for first grade. Then, the mukhtar had to go to Political Security, and they had to come and see the child.' Security operatives make this already difficult situation even more painful for some families: 'They tell us that perhaps these children are not ours, but have been smuggled in from Israel or Turkey,' the man said.

Once a maktoumeen child passes the examination at the end of grade nine, they are not issued with a diploma. Instead, they receive a substitute, inferior document which explains that the child has passed the examination and is maktoumeen. Unlike the diploma, this document is not sufficient for the purposes of moving up to grade ten and as a result, maktoumeen children struggle to pass beyond ninth grade.[25]

In addition to the specific discriminatory government policy towards education and opportunity for stateless Kurdish children, Kurdish children often have to obtain employment, working in construction, restaurants, street stalls and elsewhere in order to contribute to the family income. Although this condition is not exclusive to Kurdish children and occurs in many sections of Syrian society, the fact that Kurdish communities are predominantly poor results in this being a common predicament among Kurds and further prevents Kurdish children from obtaining equal opportunity in education.[26]

ECONOMIC DISCRIMINATION

The Kurdish areas of Syria are some of the most economically deprived areas of Syria, despite comprising some of the country's most economically productive regions. Cotton, wheat, olives, tobacco, fruits, vegetables and other products all grow easily in the rich agricultural land and the majority of oil fields and water resources are also found in these areas. Fear of losing land with such economic value to a neighbouring state or potential future Kurdish state bears heavily on the Syrian authorities. The consequences of Syria's Arabization policy – the removal of Syrian nationality, the land reforms and the resettlement of Arabs into Kurdish areas – have significantly impacted on the Kurds' economic well-being. This treatment has encouraged economic migration from the Kurdish areas, preventing Kurds from gaining a stronghold in the economy of these areas.

Public sector control of agriculture is very strong in Syria.[27] The government can and does intervene in pricing, subsidy allocations, the provision of services and the provisions of finance and loans. Such intervention can be seen particularly in the cotton and cereal farming areas of Syria, for which al-Hasakeh province is well-known.[28] Kurdish people are commonly discriminated against when applying for loans, agricultural licences or business-related licences. Because the state perceives the Kurds as a threat to national security and unity, the fact that financial applications must be subjected to security considerations causes a disproportionate number of Kurdish applications to be rejected.

Employment within the public sector is largely dependent on *wasta*, or personal connections. As a non-Arab minority, Kurds face increased difficulties in obtaining *wasta* when compared to Arabs. A key method of obtaining *wasta* is to join the Ba'th Party, but for the many Kurds who cannot deny their ethnicity as Ba'thist ideology requires, this is impossible. *Wasta* is also required for much private sector employment and for obtaining goods and services.

Many Kurds face further difficulties in obtaining employment because they have often been blacklisted for illegal political activities, even though in many cases they have not been involved in politics. Once blacklisted, an individual is barred from all public sector employment. Because the accusation that an individual is a member of a Kurdish political party can affect their employment opportunities, political party membership is often used as a tool against Kurds.

Ajanib and maktoumeen Kurds cannot obtain any public sector employment. Because the state is the main employer within Syria, this rules them out of contention for nearly all well-paid employment and they must support their families on low-paid menial work. Ajanib and maktoumeen Kurds are commonly found running street stalls in cities. In addition to the low income that these stalls generate, it is usual for the vendors to be required to regularly pay *bakshish* or bribes to local security personnel in order to keep their pitches.

EDUCATIONAL INSTITUTIONS

Education and training have a significant impact on economic opportunity. It is reported that Kurdish teachers are routinely expelled from teacher training institutes. Likewise, there are frequent reports of Kurdish students being expelled from university. During and after the Kurdish uprising in March 2005, scores of Kurdish students were thrown out of universities across Syria. In Damascus University alone, an investigative commission was formed to investigate students and more than 20 Kurdish students were expelled on 18 March 2004 in connection with their alleged participation in peaceful demonstrations. Twenty-eight students were also recalled for questioning by the commissioner under charges of 'distributing forbidden leaflets'.[29]

Ajanib and maktoumeen children, denied the full education allocated to Syrian nationals, are unable to move beyond low-paid and difficult menial work, which further impacts on the difficulties faced by many Kurdish families.

MILITARY EMPLOYMENT

Under Syrian laws, all male Syrian citizens must complete two and a half years of military service. Due to the shortage of alternative employment and the alternative of poverty, many Kurds remain in military employment beyond the minimum time. In this way, state discrimination against the Kurds has led to Kurdish dependence on one form of state employment, a form of employment which requires loyalty to the regime. Even though many Kurds remain in the army, few have advanced to officer status under the Ba'th regime. In addition, few Kurds are placed in sensitive areas of the military, such as the air force.[30] It is believed that Kurds in Syria are disproportionately positioned in the frontline of various conflicts, such as the Golan in 1973 and Lebanon since 1978.

Despite having lost citizenship in the 1962 Hasakeh census or having been born as ajanib or maktoumeen, many Kurds of ajanib or maktoumeen status have reportedly been forced to undertake military service. According to Article 40 of the Syrian Constitution, all citizens shall be required to carry out their duty in defending Syria. Furthermore, Articles 43 and 44 of the Syrian Nationality Law states that Syrian national service of two and a half years is compulsory for anyone with Syrian nationality over age 19. Despite the law clearly limiting conscription to Syrian citizens, Syria has breached its own provisions in forcing stateless Kurds to complete military service.

SUMMARY

Syrian life revolves around identity cards: travelling between states, obtaining employment, claiming state benefits and subsidies, renting hotel rooms or properties; all require identity documents. Routine identity inspections increase the obstacles to be faced for those without the correct papers. Kurds continue to report discrimination in obtaining jobs and services and economic marginalization has placed them in a position of vulnerability.

Ajanib and maktoumeen Kurds face discrimination and practical problems from birth through to death due to their lack of nationality and corresponding lack of paperwork. Although the Syrian government says that its intention in removing citizenship was to deal with 'foreigners' who had unlawfully entered the country, each successive government has failed to do anything about these alleged 'foreigners' for over 40 years. Instead of attempting to repatriate them to the countries they allegedly travelled from, or even reinstating citizenship for Kurds who could prove their nationality, the government has left these Kurds in limbo. Children born to these Kurds are placed in the same state of limbo in defiance of Syria's own nationality laws. The stateless Kurds constitute an economically, politically, and socially marginalized section of the Syrian population that is subject to daily discrimination and imposed hardship.

A further fallacy can also be seen in the Syrian government's argument that the Kurds who were affected by the 1962 census had their citizenship removed because they were foreigners who had illegally entered Syria and not entitled to citizenship. Syrian citizenship can be granted to foreign nationals after only five years' residence in Syria, but the allegedly 'foreign' Kurds who remained in Syria from 1962 to the present day have been unable to obtain citizenship in this way because they cannot show foreign nationality. Thus at the same time it describes the stateless Kurds as foreigners to deny them citizenship, the Syrian government also refuses to grant these Kurds citizenship after five years' residence because they are unable to prove they are foreign nationals – what might be called a catch-22 situation.

The denial of citizenship to ajanib and maktoumeen Kurds is a violation of domestic and international laws that guarantee citizenship and nationality to those peoples discussed above. Furthermore the act of stripping Syrian citizenship from a large proportion of the members of one ethnic group and continuing to deny it to them, as well as violating both Syrian and international laws related to nationality itself, breach numerous other clauses in both Syrian and international law that relate to freedom from racial discrimination and the rights of the child

Despite Bashar al-Asad stating publicly on more than one occasion that a solution to the condition of the stateless Kurds in Syria would be found, his comments have been in relation to around 20,000 Kurds who will apparently be given Syrian citizenship. This begs the question of what will happen to the remaining 200,000 or more Kurds without citizenship even if al-Asad's promises are carried out. Moreover, given that no action has yet been taken on restoring citizenship, the possibility of even 20,000 Kurds regaining their citizenship appears low.

9

The Political Rights
of Kurds in Syria

'Every citizen shall have the right to express his opinion publicly
and freely, in speech, writing and other forms of expression and to
participate in the work and control and the voicing of constructive
criticism aimed to ensure the safety or the structure of the Homeland
and the Nation and to enhance the socialist regime.'

Article 38, Constitution of the Syrian Arab Republic

'Citizens shall have the right of assembly and peaceful demonstration
within the principles of the Constitution and law shall regulate
this right.'

Article 39, Constitution of the Syrian Arab Republic

FREEDOM OF ASSOCIATION

Since the accession of the Ba'th Party to power in 1963 and despite
the existence of seven separate parties comprising the Progressive
National Front, the previously discussed lack of competition between
the parties means that Syria is effectively a one party state. No parties
other than those in the PNF are permitted to exist, and consequently
there are no laws governing political parties. Despite comments by
the Syrian authorities on the potential to bring in laws permitting
new political parties to join the PNF, nothing has occurred.

Although political activity is illegal outside the auspices of the
Ba'th Party or PNF, twelve Kurdish political parties operate covertly,
trying to present Kurdish demands and represent the Kurdish
section of Syrian society.[1] None of the Kurdish parties focus on the
establishment of a Kurdish state or Kurdish autonomy within Syria.
Instead, the parties seek Syrian recognition of the Kurdish population
and political representation of the Kurdish interests.

The parties are divided by several factors, including ideological
differences and the scale and openness of political activities. Because
the Syrian government has also permitted the Iraqi Kurdish KDP
and PUK parties and the Turkish Kurdish PKK party to operate on

occasion in Syria, individual Syrian Kurdish political parties are also split along party lines according to allegiance with the different external leaderships and struggles. As a result, although there is no official link between parties, Kurdish politics in Syria often reflect Kurdish party politics and divisions in Iraq and Turkey.

Political activities

Political activities in the public sphere are very limited, reflecting the fear that people have of the security services and the fear that they will be arrested for any political activity. The main activities that non-PNF parties undertake are lobbying and protest actions such as demonstrations and writing letters to the president highlighting concerns or expressing opposition to policies and arrests of individuals.

1990 parliamentary expansions saw an increased number of seats available for independent candidates; some of which were taken by Kurdish politicians, including the leaders of Syrian Kurdish political parties. However, in order to receive security clearance and be permitted to run for parliament, potential independent candidates must adhere to Ba'thist ideology, thus it is difficult for an independent Kurdish candidate to officially represent Kurdish interests.[2] Kurdish members of parliament are thus limited to addressing less crucial issues such as the provincial division of resources.

Because they are excluded from official public politics and are unable to participate in public affairs, the Kurdish political parties have limited political mandates, their agendas tending instead to focus on the private sphere of life – cultural, educational and social issues. Thus the parties can be found teaching Kurdish language and history,[3] and organizing events, intellectual debates, traditional festivals, weddings, sports and other cultural events. In this way they contribute to the maintenance of Kurdish culture for future generations.

FREEDOM OF ASSEMBLY

Under Article 21 of the International Covenant on Civil and Political Rights (hereafter 'ICCPR'), the right to peaceful assembly shall be recognized and no restrictions may be placed on the exercise of this right other than those necessary in a democratic society.

The Syrian Constitution states that people have the right to meet and demonstrate peacefully within the principles of the Constitution and as regulated by law.[4] However, the law that 'regulates the exercise of this right' is emergency law given the Constitution's inferiority to the state of emergency laws. This subordination permits state of emergency laws to impose draconian restrictions on freedom of association, assembly and demonstration. A further problem with the stipulation in the Constitution is that Kurdish protests including a demand for the recognition of the Kurdish nation in Syria can be condemned and its participants arrested, on the basis that they challenge the Arab character of the people, incite sectarian strife and threaten the unity of the state.

Demonstrations are frequently met with police violence and arrests. The small numbers of people attending demonstrations in Damascus reflect the harsh punishments that are meted out for political actions that confront the state or Ba'th regime. For Kurdish political parties, protests and demonstrations are the main ways they can draw attention to the situation of stateless Kurds, non-recognition of the Kurdish community or language in Syria, and the problems faced in forming cultural or sports clubs and associations. Yet the majority of Kurdish protests are met with the arrests of many individuals and forcible dispersion of protesters.

Kurdish protests and demonstrations did not occur prior to March 1990, when several Kurds were elected as independent candidates to the Syrian parliament. Encouraged by this, many Kurds staged a demonstration against the denial of citizenship to *ajanib* and *maktoumeen* Kurds. This first demonstration ended when the protesters attempted to present the president with a list of demands.[5]

Over the years, although state suppression of demonstrations has continued, international events such as the intervention in Iraq in the early 1990s and repeated intervention in 2003 have given Kurdish political parties a renewed degree of confidence, causing them to become more vocal. US-led intervention in Iraq in March 2003 and the gains made by the Kurds in Iraqi Kurdistan influenced Kurdish confidence in Syria significantly, contributing to the general political confidence among Kurds in Syria. Although an increased number of demonstrations and public protests have occurred more recently, few large-scale demonstrations were seen until the events of March 2004 in Qamishli.

On 10 December 2002 – International Human Rights Day – approximately 150 *Partîya Yekîtî Kurdî li Sûriye* members demonstrated outside the Syrian parliament. Their slogans and placards called for citizenship to be granted to Kurds, a removal of the ban on Kurdish language and demanded respect for human rights in Syria. This demonstration was one of the first major demonstrations since the Ba'th Party came to power.

After attending the demonstration, two members of the party leadership, Hasan Salih and Marwan 'Uthman were later arrested and charged with belonging to a secret organization and with inciting religious and ethnic strife. By October 2003, this charge had been altered to the crime of attempting to sever a part of the Syrian state and annex it to a foreign country. The two men were released from prison on 22 February 2004.

On 25 June 2003, approximately 380 children attended a peace march to the UNICEF building in Damascus to mark World Children's Day, carrying flowers and banners asking for freedom of cultural expression and language and human rights. Before the children reached their destination, more than 400 security personnel intervened and forcibly dispersed the crowd, arresting seven men.

The seven men were tried in the Syrian State Security Court on 27 June 2004, charged with 'belonging to a secret organisation' and, 'attempting to sever part of the Syrian territory and annex it to a foreign state'. According to Amnesty International, their trial was unfair. All seven were sentenced to five years, which was reduced to between one and two years, allowing the four men sentenced to one year to be released having already served their time.[6]

On International Human Rights Day 2003, again on 10 December, Kurdish parties and Syrian human rights organizations participated in a further demonstration demanding the respect of international human rights standards and rights for all Syria's citizens. Between 300 and 1,200[7] people gathered in front of the Syrian parliament and attempted to present a petition signed by Arab and Kurdish democracy activists, advocates and political party representatives. However, in contrast to the policy adopted in recent demonstrations, the Prime Minister, Naji al-'Utari refused to accept the petition.

Disproportionate force against demonstrators occurred again in March 2004 following the deaths of several Kurds in Qamishli.[8] When thousands of Kurds took to the streets to protest the deaths and general oppression of the Ba'th Party, they were met with military force. The police, security services and military forces used live ammunition and shrapnel bullets to quell demonstrations, inflicting bullet-related injuries on hundreds of Kurds. Many then received inadequate medical treatment because they were arrested and detained prior to obtaining treatment, or because security personnel had insisted that injured persons be treated in state hospitals where there were insufficient facilities to treat all the wounded.[9] Suppression of the demonstrations was justified on the grounds of preserving Syrian unity. Hundreds of Kurds were arrested during and after the demonstrations and by early 2005 many Kurds remained in detention, having not yet been tried for any alleged offences.[10]

Arrests and detention

Although people do not 'disappear' in Syria on the same scale as disappearances of the 1980s and although political detentions have also decreased, there are still many prisoners of conscience in Syrian jails. Many events have contributed to the number of individuals currently detained for their political opinions: the arrests of civil society and human rights activities in the 2001 crackdown on the Damascus Spring movement; arrests of individuals accused of having connections to the banned Muslim Brotherhood; the arrests of many Kurds during the buildup to and aftermath of the 2003 Iraq War; and the uprising of March 2004, following which many hundreds of Kurds were arrested. Although many of these Kurds were released soon after their initial arrest, alleging they had been tortured, many Kurds remain in detention or are unaccounted for.[11] Reports suggest that more than 20 Kurdish children between the ages of 13 and 17 were arrested in the March 2004 protests, several of whom had not even been in the vicinity of the unrest. Some of these children are known to have been subjected to torture while in detention.[12]

Kurds can be arrested for both cultural and political activities in Syria. Activities such as writing, distributing and even reading information on Kurdish culture and history are deemed to be political and can lead to arrest. Kurds arrested and detained for such 'crimes' are often subjected to torture or ill-treatment. It is believed that family members of political activists have often been arrested merely because of their association with the detainee, and family members of both political activists and exiles are reportedly intimidated. These tactics of intimidation and setting examples of individual families are intended to prevent others from becoming involved in political activity.

On 8 August 2003, Khalil Mustafa was arrested for his political beliefs[13] and subjected to severe torture while in detention. Khalil is believed to have died in custody on 10 August 2003. Although his body was handed over to his family, the village *mukhabarat* prevented them from burying Khalil in his home village as is customary. Instead, the family was forced to bury him in Aleppo.[14] After al-

Jazeera and other media stations broadcast information on Khalil's death, prompting the political security forces (*al-Amn al-Siyassi*) to come and question Khalil's relatives, his brother Hasan Mustafa was arrested on 18 October 2003. Hasan was held incommunicado at an unknown location until his release on 30 January 2004, when he required medical treatment for the after effects of the torture he had suffered whilst in custody.[15]

During 2003 and 2004, trials of political detainees have often been accompanied by demonstrations outside the court building and delegations of lawyers and representatives of many European consulates have attended the proceedings. It is believed that the release of Marwan 'Uthman and Hasan Salih on 22 February 2004 was secured partly by the involvement of international NGOs[16] and representatives of European governments in their case. While international pressures on Syria are extracting a degree of transparency in the judicial proceedings in more high profile cases such as these, the arrest and lengthy detention of Kurds with no international or internal pressure networks or support go unreported. It is common for a layperson to be detained in prison for more than five years for an offence such as possessing Kurdish written material of a 'political' nature.

FREEDOM OF EXPRESSION

The press

Under the 1965 Revolution Protection Law, offences considered to violate the implementation of the socialist state system are punishable by lifelong hard labour. Offences of this sort are not restricted to deeds but include word of mouth or writing, or any other form of expression or publication.[17] This law provides a good introduction to the severely limited press freedom within Syria. Publications in Kurdish were initially banned, seized and destroyed by then-President Adib al-Shishakli between 1951 and 1954, and were banned again from 1958 to 1961, during the years of the United Arab Republic. This prohibition on Kurdish publications continues under the Ba'th Party today.

All Syrian newspapers are official or semi-official, representing the parties of the Progressive National Front. Within newspapers, only the official opinion supporting Ba'th Party policy is permitted to be published. Because working for the press in Syria requires a permit obtainable from the Ministry of Information and security forces, many journalists are prevented from working or have their requests for permits denied due to alleged impartial covering of Syrian policies.[18]

Under a 2001 Publication Act, the Prime Minister, at the request of the Ministry of Information, may cancel a permit granted to any newspaper, magazine or publication; furthermore, in doing so the Prime Minister is not required to provide reasons for doing so. At least 15 permits have been cancelled since 2000 due to the conditions and complications imposed on publications. One newspaper, *Al Domari*, faced many obstacles prior to having its permit cancelled by the Prime Minister in July 2003; many of these obstacles were caused by the former Minister of Information Adnan Umran.[19]

Although officially independent newspapers are now allowed, closer inspection reveals that this is not the case. For example *Abyad wa Aswad*, sold as an independent political magazine, is owned by the son of the new Syrian Defence Minister.[20]

Decree Number 50

Prior to 2001, the 1949 General Law on Printed Matter covered all aspects of printing and publishing. In 2001, Decree 50 was passed by the Syrian government as a replacement for the 1949 law. Applying to publishers, printers, journalists, editors, authors, distributors and bookshop owners, the Decree consists of over 50 articles, all aimed at restricting print media freedom and increasing state control. Human rights organizations have condemned the Decree for 'keeping the Syrian media in the Stone Age'.[21]

The Decree lays out the requirements for licensing, ownership and operation of print publications. It outlines information that must be provided to the government on a daily basis and restricts a variety of subjects from being published. Finally, the Decree sets out the punishments for violation of any of its regulations.

According to Article 16, only Arab Syrian nationals may own or manage publishing houses and printing presses. Under the new law, the Prime Minister can deny licences to both publishers and printers for any reason related to the public interest. The government is authorized to monitor all publications. Under Article 8, printing companies must provide copies of any printed material to the Syrian ministry of Information on the day of printing. By requiring printers and publishers to provide information including the date of printing, identity of the printing company and number of copies printed, printers and publishers take on responsibility for all published material.

Article 9 permits the Ministry of Information to ban a publication and punish the printers, distributors and sellers if the publication infringes upon national security or offends public morality.[22] If the law is violated, harsh prison sentences and heavy fines can be imposed on printers and publishers. These punishments can be imposed if published material is linked to the instigation of, or praise for crimes;[23] if a report is deemed to be fabricated;[24] or if the published material is deemed to harm the public interest, national security or national unity.[25] These crimes are not clearly defined and this vagueness places a heavy burden on authors, editors, publishers and distributors. If their interpretation of the law is different to the current interpretation taken by the authorities, they face harsh punishment. They consequently practise self-censorship, erring on the side of caution and not publishing material that might in any way be unacceptable to the authorities. The law thus has the effect of stifling freedom of expression within the Syrian press and publication sector.

This lack of free expression has a disproportionate effect on the Kurdish section of the Syrian population by denying them access to Kurdish press and publications. Kurdish publications may be deemed to seek constitutional change or to threaten national unity by association with Kurdish demands for national recognition. Because Kurdish cultural expression is a political issue within Syria, even clearly 'innocent' Kurdish cultural publications may go unpublished. Besides the unwillingness of publishers to print and distribute Kurdish materials, many Kurds have been arrested merely for possessing or distributing Kurdish publications. In early 2002 Ibrahim Nasan, a Kurdish author, was arrested and imprisoned for distributing cultural and educational material in the Kurdish language.[26]

The net result of this is that authors and publishers who do wish to publish Kurdish material in Syria are instead forced to send their work for publication in neighbouring countries such as Lebanon and then risk smuggling the finished work back into Syria.

Television

All television and satellite stations are under state ownership, belonging to the 'General Corporation for Broadcasting and TV'. On 15 March 2004 Abdul-Razzaq Salim, reporter for Al Arabiyya Satellite Channel, was arrested whilst covering the events in Qamishli during the Kurdish demonstrations. His audio and video tapes were confiscated and he was released several days later with a warning.[27]

The internet in Syria

Despite online connection that was established back in 1997, internet access is limited to a privileged minority of no more than 80,000 people throughout Syria.[28] Online content is filtered and email closely monitored. On 24 July 2003, 29-year-old Kurdish journalism student, Massud Hamid was arrested whilst sitting an exam at Damascus University. His arrest came after photographs were posted on <www.amude.com> of the peaceful Kurdish demonstration in June 2003 outside UNICEF headquarters in Damascus. He was given a three-year prison sentence in October 2004, after having already spent 14 months in prison where he was reportedly subjected to mistreatment.[29] Other individuals who have written for internet sites have been accused of 'publishing false information outside Syria'.[30]

Syria's two internet service providers are both government-controlled. The state-run Syrian Telecommunications Establishment filters hundreds of websites which it deems to be pornographic, pro-Israeli or critical of the regime. For example, access to the website of the Syrian Human Rights Committee has been blocked for several years.[31] Access to two Kurdish websites, <www.amude.com> and <www.qamislo.com>, was blocked in mid-March 2004; the sites, which are run from Germany, had shown news, pictures and video clips about demonstrations by the Kurdish minority.[32]

Although Bashar al-Asad is said to be the country's most prominent advocate of the internet, it is reported that his interest in allowing public internet access has been opposed by security and intelligence officials.[33]

SUMMARY

Despite apparent reforms, press freedom remains extremely limited in Syria, due to the high level of state control imposed on it. Use of the internet is so limited that few Syrians can access it to research or publish information. Even in the field of publications, where Syrian law does not explicitly prohibit publishing in languages other than Arabic, the fear of prosecution for a 'political offence' means that most publishers and printers are reluctant to publish Kurdish material. Since Decree 50 was passed, this reluctance has increased as people attempt to avoid the revocation of publishing licences, heavy fines or prison sentences. This total clampdown on publication and press freedom has had a disproportionate effect on the Kurdish section of Syrian society by denying them access to Kurdish publications and newspapers.

Their freedom of expression, assembly and association suppressed by the state, Kurds in Syria are effectively denied a political platform from which to raise their problems. The authorities justify this by arguing that Kurdish political expression is linked to separatist intentions or that the Kurds may be exploited by 'foreign parties' that are hostile to the Syrian state and Ba'th Party. By adhering to nationalist political rhetoric and defining the Syrian state as being ethnically and nationally Arab, Kurdish interests are excluded from social, economic and political accommodation, denying the opportunity for meaningful political representation of Syria's largest minority group.

10
Kurdish Cultural Rights

'In those states in which ethnic, religious or linguistic minorities exist, persons belonging to such minorities shall not be denied the right, in community with other members of their group, to enjoy their own culture, to profess and practice their religion, or to use their own language.' Article 27, International Covenant on Civil and Political Rights; Article 30, Convention on the Rights of the Child; Article 2, Declaration on the Rights of Persons belonging to National or Ethnic, Religious and Linguistic Minorities (1992)

'Minorities shall not be deprived of their right to enjoy their culture or to follow the teachings of their religions.' Article 37, Arab Charter of Human Rights

Nations define themselves through the notion of shared languages, culture and history. Within states, different communities may use different languages and follow a range of cultural activities to define themselves as belonging to their specific group. The rights of minority groups to enjoy their culture, practise their religions and use their own languages are viewed with such fundamental importance that they are protected by international legal covenants, including the International Covenant on Civil and Political Rights. Closer to Syria, the Arab Charter of Human Rights also protects the right of minority groups to enjoy their culture.

As a group constituting an ethnic minority in Syria, Iraq, Iran, Turkey and republics of the former Soviet Union, the Kurds therefore fall under the protection of these international and regional instruments and should be free to enjoy the many facets of Kurdish culture: its language, history, traditions and religions. Unfortunately, as with civil and political rights, Syria makes the enjoyment of Kurdish culture difficult, if not impossible, for many of the Kurds within its borders.

Syrian restrictions exist on the use and practice of the Kurdish language, reflecting the practices also found in Turkey, Iraq and Iran at various points during recent history. The policy of suppressing

Kurdish language and culture is intended to forcibly assimilate the Kurds into the majority culture of the respective country; within Turkey, the Kurds are described as Turkish; within Syria, the aim is to assimilate the Kurds to the Arab culture and identity.

THE KURDISH LANGUAGE

After the French Mandate ended without the French securing guarantees for Kurdish cultural rights, the Kurds began to face increasing numbers of measures intended to prevent the teaching and learning of Kurdish. As a result of these restrictions, many Kurds speak both Kurdish and Arabic in urban areas such as Damascus, although Kurmanji remains the main language of Kurds in northern Syria. As mentioned previously, Kurdish knowledge of Arabic is also limited by the fact that most Kurdish children do not begin to learn Arabic until the age of five.

Despite there being a sizeable minority Kurdish population in Syria, Kurdish is not recognized as an official language. It is not taught in schools and when Kurds with Syrian citizenship qualify as teachers, they are not permitted to speak Kurdish whilst on the schools' premises. Even if parents wish their children to study the Kurdish language, the authorities do not permit private language schools to teach Kurdish. In contrast, other minority groups including the Armenians, Circassians and Assyrians have been able to open private language schools. As a result of this, Kurdish can only be taught informally in private houses.[1]

The printing and distribution of Kurdish books and other materials is extremely difficult. Kurdish groups pay large sums for books to be printed secretly or instead illegally import Kurdish books from Lebanon and northern Iraq.

Decree Number 1012/S/25, issued in 1986, forbade the use of Kurdish in the workplace, cinemas and cafes.[2] Other decrees have continued to limit the use of languages other than Arabic.[3]

Many towns and villages in the predominantly Kurdish regions of Syria have also been affected by the ban on the Kurdish language. From the 1970s onwards, the names of many Kurdish villages were changed to Arabic under directives such as Directive No. 15801 of May 1977, under which the minister of local administration ordered that the Kurdish names of many towns and villages in Afrin region, Aleppo governorate, be replaced with Arabic names. Thus, Kobaniya is now 'Ain al-'Arab, Girdeem is now Sa'diyya, Chilara is now Jowadiyya and so forth.[4]

From 1992 onwards, the ban on Kurdish language widened to even include Kurdish names, as the authorities of Hasakeh province began refusing to register children with Kurdish names. This resulted from orders by the Minister of the Interior that any parents who wished to give their child a non-Arab name must obtain approval from the local security forces. The reason given for this was that the Arabic alphabet does not contain certain sounds contained within other languages; however this policy has had a disproportionate effect on the Kurdish population.[5]

In 1994, Hasakeh's governor Subhi Harb, gave owners of Kurdish-named businesses one week in which to change the name of the business to Arabic. He ordered the city and town councils of the region not to issue permits to shops, hotels, restaurants and other businesses if they used Kurdish names and to threaten closure and prosecution to existing Kurdish-named businesses if they failed to change the business name. On a 1995 trip to Syria, Human Rights Watch saw signs in Arabic, Armenian and Russian, but none in Kurdish.[6]

When Human Rights Watch asked the Syrian government in 1996 to explain the issues raised above relating to the Kurdish language, the government failed to respond to many of the issues raised, responding only to the issue of the ban on Kurdish in the workplace,

> the Syrian Constitution stipulates that Syria is part pf the greater Arab nation and that Arabic is its official language. It stipulates further that the ban on the use of foreign languages in the workplace is not limited to the Kurdish language but includes all languages other than Arabic.

and noting that certain letters in other alphabets such as Kurdish were not included in the Arabic alphabet.[7]

Whilst the government may be able to argue the existence of a legitimate interest in using only Arabic names for businesses, the fact that other languages than Kurdish were still permitted shows they apply this policy in a discriminatory manner. Likewise, the fact that Kurdish language schools and clubs are prohibited whilst Armenian, Assyrian and even French or English language schools exist serves only to highlight the discriminatory application of official policies.

Under Article 4(3) of the 1992 Declaration on the Rights of Persons Belonging to National or Ethnic, Religious and Linguistic Minorities, states should take appropriate measures so that, wherever possible, persons belonging to minorities may have adequate opportunities to learn their mother tongue or to have instruction in their mother tongue. Although not legally binding, the fact that Syrian practices completely contradict the recommended approach demonstrates the lack of respect accorded to the Kurds in Syria.

TRADITION

A key Kurdish tradition is *Newroz*, which celebrates the Kurdish New Year on 21 March. The festival also represents the victory of the oppressed over tyranny: according to legend, over 2,500 years ago the Kurds were ruled by King Zuhak, who one day grew two serpents from his shoulders. To prevent them eating his brain, King Zuhak fed the brains of two children to the serpents each day. Eventually Kawa, a brave blacksmith who had lost several of his children in this way, led a rebellion against Zuhak, using fires on hill tops as a signal for others to join together and defeat the King. After Zawa defeated Zuhak, the people celebrated their new freedom.

In keeping with the legend, Newroz is usually celebrated with large bonfires on hill tops, where people dress in the Kurdish colours and sing and dance. To the Kurds, Newroz represents the passing of winter, the coming of a new year and also represents freedom, life and revolution.

Given Syria's general antipathy towards the Kurds, it is easy to see that Newroz causes tension each year, as it also does in Turkey. As a result, it has periodically been forbidden in Syria and even when permitted is subject to many restrictions. Kurds are often prevented from wearing the Kurdish colours of red, yellow and green and are also often prevented from travelling to celebrations.[8] During celebrations, Syrian police and security forces form a heavy presence in the Kurdish areas and the size of Newroz celebrations in each area is dependent upon the discretion of provincial governors and security offices.[9]

In 1986, the Newroz festival saw large scale Kurdish demonstrations in Damascus interrupted by the police opening fire, causing the death of a young boy. Other Kurds were arrested following the events in Damascus and elsewhere, including in Afrin, where several Kurds were killed when the police attempted to disperse celebrators and protestors.[10] Following these events, Hafiz al-Asad passed a decree declaring 21 March to be Mothers Day; allegedly believing that by turning 21 March into an Arab national holiday, tensions would be defused. Unfortunately, tensions still exist, as was seen during the 1995 Newroz festival. The festival had been prohibited that year, allegedly due to the death of Hafiz al-Asad's son in a car crash the previous year. When Kurds began to gather in order to celebrate their festival, around 60 were arrested by Syrian police. Arrests occurred again in 1997 when the authorities accused several Kurds of distributing Kurdish nationalist songs.[11]

The most recent Newroz celebrations have been more subdued: 2003, due to the ongoing Iraq war and 2004, out of respect to the many Kurds killed, injured or arrested the previous week following the events in Qamishli.

MUSIC

A core element of Kurdish culture, music has been targeted by the authorities for over 50 years. As early as 1954, Kurdish gramophone recordings and publications were seized and their owners detained following the overthrow of Adib al-Shishakli.[12] An order issued in 1987 by the Culture Minister, Najar al-'Attar, forbade the playing and circulation of Kurdish music and videos, although the enforcement of this policy has relaxed somewhat over the years and Kurdish music is now tolerated in Kurdish towns and quarters of urban areas. Even so, the music on sale is still restricted, as sellers and distributors still face imprisonment if they sell Kurdish music which could be perceived as being political or nationalist in nature. The singing of non-Arabic songs at weddings and festivals was prohibited by Decree 1865/S/25 in December 1989.[13] Tolerance of Kurdish music seems to depend on the political climate in the region so that, during the buildup to the 2003 Iraq War, increased restrictions were seen.

SUMMARY

Although Kurds continue to refer to towns and villages by their traditional Kurdish names, a part of the town's Kurdish character has been forever lost by the new Arabic name. The Kurdish history that the original name evoked has effectively been wiped from the official Syrian consciousness though its Arabization policy. The state authorities benefit because they can more easily argue that the Kurds migrated from Turkey and Iraq to settle in Syria, since the loss of a town's Kurdish name and identity makes it more difficult for Kurds to claim a historical presence in the region as inhabitants as opposed to a migrant population.

This insistence that the Kurds are a migrant population is further bolstered by the state's denial of Kurdish history in the region. Kurdish individuals have played their part in the rich tapestry that makes up Syrian history: they have helped to form governments; they have participated in the army and in other professions; and they have contributed in the development of Syrian society. Yet barely any mention is made of them in Syrian history books and they are instead described as a migrant group. The removal of Kurdish place names provides an additional benefit to the state by bolstering its argument that the Kurds form a non-native group within Syria; the lack of Kurdish-named areas proves there was no historical Kurdish presence, according to the state. However, this official line is contradicted by authors such as Basile Nikitine.[14]

The prohibition on expressions of Kurdish identity is a feature shared by all states with Kurdish inhabitants. The Kurds have responded by clinging to whatever shreds of cultural identity they can in order to preserve their heritage, but this serves only to increase suspicions about Kurdish intentions, causing even harsher suppression. Within Syria this suppression, when combined with the existence of a state security and intelligence network that pervades all aspects of daily life, has succeeded in creating a fear of any public expression of Kurdish cultural identity.

Conclusion

The consequences of the official Arabization policies of the 1960s and 1970s continue to have serious implications today. As the Syrian government has failed to reverse the effects of the 1962 census, the ramifications of the census worsen each year as more children are born to stateless Kurds and the stateless Kurdish population increases. Although the Arab Belt policy was suspended in 1976, the villages built under the policy are still standing and the relocated Arab migrants and displaced Kurds remain where they were sent in the 1970s. Biased redistribution of land taken from Kurdish landowners was never corrected and many formerly wealthy landowners lost both their lands and nationality overnight.

The Hasakeh census, Arab Belt policy and associated land reforms have all combined to alter the demographic structure of Kurdish regions in Syria and remove the dominance of Kurds in the Jazira, an area rich in natural resources. The perceived threat of separatism caused the Syrian authorities to implement enforced disintegration of Kurdish communities, whilst failed attempts to assimilate the Kurds with Arab Syrians simply resulted in further 'dilution' of the Kurdish regions. Land reforms across the Kurdish areas of Syria have succeeded in establishing physical divisions between once contiguous Kurdish communities.

Stripping Kurds of their citizenship and land and placing obstacles in the path of education and employment has had a negative socio-economic effect on the Kurds in Syria. Kurds affected by these policies, both directly or though inheriting their consequences, are largely impoverished and consequently unable to alter their economic, legal or social status. This has led to mass urban migration from Kurdish areas to cities as families attempt to cling to their property in the north by sending their children to cities such as Damascus and Aleppo to find menial work and an income with which to support their families, further reducing the Kurdish population in traditionally Kurdish areas of Syria. Whole new areas in the outskirts of Damascus have been built illegally by Kurdish migrants, primarily from al-Hasakeh province because they cannot buy or rent property anywhere in Syria.[1]

Many other Kurds have left Syria to find a better quality of life and reported encouragement of Kurds to leave Syria by those connected with the Ba'th regime further impacts on the Kurdish population in Syria. By failing to address the many problems affecting the Kurdish population in Syria, Syria fails to meet international and domestic standards.

Regionally, all of Syria, Iraq, Turkey and Iran have used the Kurds as tools against their neighbours, whilst working together on the shared interest of preventing Kurdish gains in one state on the grounds that they would necessarily affect the demands and aspirations of Kurds in another. Iraqi Kurdish support for the US-led invasion of Iraq and the inclusion of the Iraqi Kurds in the centre of the political process of determining the future of Iraq have increased anti-Kurdish policy and sentiment within the ruling regime in Syria and among its Arab majority. Both aid to and discrimination against the Kurds regionally has affected the situation for the Kurds of Syria.

Since Bashar al-Asad came to power in 2000, regional and international events have also conspired to place Syria in an increasingly delicate position and have had a significant effect on Syrian foreign and domestic policy. The international war on terror, the 2003 Iraq War and events in the Lebanon have redefined Syria's relations with both the West and its neighbours in the Middle East. US policy has shifted from 'constructive engagement' with Syria to public calls for Syrian accountability and compliance with the US Middle Eastern agenda, drawing Syria to the forefront of Western attention.

Recent events have also served to reinforce Ba'th Party perceptions that Syria is under threat from the West and other states in the region, and that these external forces are already working within Syria by fomenting political dissent. This perception of increased threat has thus far served only to further entrench Syria's 'hardliners' and the 'old-guard', further thwarting democratization. Associating the Kurds with these external forces has also reinforced the belief that the Kurds are a potential threat to the Syrian state and Ba'th regime, placing the Kurds under increased measures aimed at protecting the unity of the state and Arab nation. The increasing numbers of Kurds arrested in recent years is testimony that hardliners in Syria are attempting to reassert their hold over the country, and that reform in Syria is by no means democratization.

This book has shown that the Kurds of Syria face particular forms of discrimination in Syria solely on the basis of their ethnic identity, which the Syrian state cannot or will not accommodate. Despite public overtures made by Bashar al-Asad, little has been done to resolve this discrimination. Although until now, international attention has been fixed on the Kurds of Iraq, current events in Iraq, Lebanon and changing US policy may finally serve to shift this focus across to the Kurds of Syria.

Although many of these incidents are still too recent to predict what effect they will have either domestically within Syria, or on the Middle East region overall, it is clear that there will be some repercussions. Noting recent Iraqi and Palestinian elections, Israeli–Palestinian peace talks and peaceful demonstrations in Lebanon, there have been claims that democracy has arrived in the Middle East, heralding a new era for the region. However, it is too early to make this claim: despite Iraqi elections, there still remains resistance to the concept of a permanent Kurdish autonomous region in northern Iraq; despite anti-Syrian demonstrations in Lebanon there were also larger, pro-Syrian demonstrations organized by Hezbollah, indicating that Syrian troop redeployment could cause instability in the region.

The key question is how Bashar al-Asad amends Syrian foreign and domestic policy to reflect recent events. If Syria concedes too much externally, al-Asad knows that internal demands may increase. At the same time, if Syria does not concede externally, the US has made it clear that further action will be taken. The question is how Bashar al-Asad will react. He could refuse to concede to international demands, risking international action (whether by sanctions, force or other means) against Syria which may negatively affect the Kurdish population.

Alternatively, al-Asad could concede to international demands regarding Lebanon whilst pre-empting potential domestic disturbance by providing token gestures such as the return of citizenship to a few thousand Kurds. In this way he can claim that he is dealing with domestic abuses of human rights and thus deflect international attention elsewhere, whilst in fact the token granting of citizenship to a small proportion of the stateless Kurds would not sufficiently deal with the situation of the Kurds in Syria.

However, if the Kurds in Syria take advantage of the current situation to highlight their concerns and the lack of minority rights, it will be more difficult for al-Asad to take a course of action that does not adequately deal with the provision of such rights. If the international community is made fully aware of the daily problems suffered by Kurds in Syria, any action taken by al-Asad is likely to face deeper scrutiny to ensure it resolves Kurdish concerns.

Appendix 1
Extract from Treaty of Sèvres

SECTION III: KURDISTAN

Article 62

A Commission sitting at Constantinople and composed of three members appointed by the British, French and Italian Governments respectively shall draft within six months from the coming into force of the present Treaty a scheme of local autonomy for the predominantly Kurdish areas lying east of the Euphrates, south of the southern boundary of Armenia as it may be hereafter determined, and north of the frontier of Turkey with Syria and Mesopotamia, as defined in Article 27, II (2) and (3). If unanimity cannot be secured on any question, it will be referred by the members of the Commission to their respective Governments. The scheme shall contain full safeguards for the protection of the Assyro-Chaldeans and other racial or religious minorities within these areas, and with this object a Commission composed of British, French, Italian, Persian and Kurdish representatives shall visit the spot to examine and decide what rectifications, if any, should be made in the Turkish frontier where, under the provisions of the present Treaty, that frontier coincides with that of Persia.

Article 63

The Turkish Government hereby agrees to accept and execute the decisions of both the Commissions mentioned in Article 62 within three months from their communication to the said Government.

Article 64

If within one year from the coming into force of the present Treaty the Kurdish peoples within the areas defined in Article 62 shall address themselves to the Council of the League of Nations in such a manner as to show that a majority of the population of these areas desires independence from Turkey, and if the Council then considers that these peoples are capable of such independence and recommends that it should be granted to them, Turkey hereby agrees to execute such a recommendation, and to renounce all rights and title over these areas.

The detailed provisions for such renunciation will form the subject of a separate agreement between the Principal Allied Powers and Turkey.

If and when such renunciation takes place, no objection will be raised by the Principal Allied Powers to the voluntary adhesion to such an independent Kurdish State of the Kurds inhabiting that part of Kurdistan which has hitherto been included in the Mosul vilayet.

Appendix 2
Syria's International
Law Obligations

Syria is a party to the international instruments which make provision to ensure respect for human dignity and basic human rights. Those to which it is party include the following:

Universal Declaration of Human Rights, adopted by the General Assembly Resolution 217A(III) on 10 December 1948.

International Covenant on Civil and Political Rights (CCPR), of 16 December 1966, (acceded to by the Syrian Arab Republic on 23 March 1976).

International Covenant on Economic, Social and Cultural Rights (CESCR), of 16 December 1966 (acceded to by the Syrian Arab Republic 3 January 1976).

The International Convention on the Elimination of All Forms of Racial Discrimination (CERD), of 31 December 1965 (acceded to by the Syrian Arab Republic 21 May 1969).

Convention on the Elimination of All Forms of Discrimination against Women (CEDAW), of 1 March 1980 (acceded to by the Syrian Arab Republic on 27 April 2003).

Convention against Torture and other Cruel, Inhuman or Degrading Treatment or Punishment (CAT), of 10 December 1984 (acceded to by the Syrian Arab Republic on 18 September 2004).

The International Convention on the Suppression and Punishment of the Crime of Apartheid of 30 November 1973 (signed by the Syrian Arab Republic on 17 January 1974, ratified on 18 November 1988).

The International Convention against Apartheid in Sports, of 10 December 1985 (signed by the Syrian Arab Republic on 16 May 1986, ratified on 28 November 1988).

The Convention on the Prevention and Punishment of the Crime of Genocide, of 9 December 1948 (acceded to by the Syrian Arab Republic on 25 June 1955).

The Convention on the Rights of the Child (CRC), of 30 November 1989 (signed by the Syrian Arab Republic on 18 September 1990, ratified on 14 April 1993).

Optional Protocol to the Convention on the Rights of the Child on the involvement of Children in Armed Conflict (acceded to by the Syrian Arab Republic on 17 November 2003).

Optional Protocol to the Convention on the Rights of the Child on the sale of children, Child Prostitution and Child Pornography (acceded to by the Syrian Arab Republic on 15 June 2003).

The Slavery Convention, of 25 September 1926; *Protocol of 1953 amending the Convention of 1926; The Slavery Convention of 1926, as amended* (signed by the Syrian Arab Republic on 4 August 1954).

The Supplementary Convention on the Abolition of Slavery, the Slave Trade, and Institutions and Practices Similar to Slavery, of 7 September 1956 (acceded to by the Syrian Arab Republic on 17 April 1958).

The four *Geneva Conventions* of 1949 and the *First Additional Protocol* of 1977.

OTHER RELEVANT INSTITUTIONS AND CONVENTIONS

The Arab Charter on Human Rights, 1994, by the League of Arab states, of which Syria is a member.

The *Organisation of the Islamic Conference*, which adopted the *Cairo Declaration on Human Rights in Islam* in 1990. Although it is not formerly binding to governments it represents a political commitment to uphold and respect human rights and the freedom of expression.

The adoption of the *Barcelona Declaration* in 27–28 November 1995 by fifteen countries of the European Union and twelve southern Mediterranean countries, including Syria, established the *Euro-Mediterranean Partnership*. Primarily a partnership to enhance economic, political and cultural relations between its members, it also calls for a commitment to respect basic human rights and freedoms.

The *Sana'a Declaration on Promoting an Independent and Pluralistic Arab Media* of 11 January 1996, sponsored by UNESCO and endorsed by UNESCO's General Conference in November 1997. Syria endorsed the principles and recommendations of the declaration at the conference.

Notes

1 THE KURDS

1. Izady, Mehrdad (1992), *The Kurds: A Concise Handbook* (USA: Taylor & Francis Inc.), page 32.
2. Izady, Prof. M.R., 'Kurdish History and Culture', taken from a lecture given at Harvard University (10 March 1983).
3. See *Encyclopaedia of Kurdistan* available at <www.kurdistanica.com>.
4. Izady, 'Kurdish History and Culture'.
5. Ibid.
6. Ibid.
7. Izady, Mehrdad, 'Exploring Kurdish Origins', lecture published in *Kurdish Life* No.5, Summer (1983).
8. Nezan, Kendal, 'A Brief Survey of the History of the Kurds', presented to the International Paris Conference 'The Kurds: Human Rights and Cultural Identity' (14–18 October 1989), available in *Collated Contributions & Messages* published by Institut Kurde de Paris (March 1992), page 31.
9. See Map 2.
10. Cook, Helena (1995), *The Safe Haven in Northern Iraq* (London: University of Essex Human Rights Centre & KHRP).
11. Yildiz, Kerim, and Deborah Russo (2000), *Azerbaijan and Armenia: An Update on Ethnic Minorities and Human Rights* (London: KHRP), page 1.
12. McDowall, David (2000), *A Modern History of the Kurds* (London: I.B. Tauris), page 6.
13. Ibid.
14. See Chapter 6, 'Water Resources and Conflict', for more information on conflict over the Euphrates and Tigris rivers. See also Kurdish Human Rights Project (2001), *If the River Were a Pen: The Ilisu Dam, the World Commission on Dams and Export Credit Reform* (London: KHRP); Kurdish Human Rights Project (2002), *Downstream Impacts of Turkish Dam Construction on Syria and Iraq* (London: KHRP); Kurdish Human Rights Project (2003), *This is the Only Valley Where I Live: The Impact of the Munzur Dam* (London: KHRP).
15. See KHRP, *Downstream Impacts of Turkish Dam Construction on Syria and Iraq*.
16. Meaning 'religious community' or 'people,' *millet* was used in Ottoman Turkey to refer to an autonomous religious community. Taken from *Encyclopaedia Britannica* available at <www.britannica.com>.
17. Meaning 'reorganization', *tanzimat* reforms were a series of reforms promulgated in the Ottoman Empire between 1839 and 1876 under the reigns of the sultans Abdülmecid I and Abdülaziz. See *Encyclopaedia Britannica* available at <www.britannica.com>.
18. Gurâni is also the sacred language of adherents to the Ahl-I Haqq sect (see 'Religion' section below).

130 The Kurds in Syria

19. McDowall, *Modern History of the Kurds*, page 10.
20. Izady, *The Kurds*, page 167.
21. Izady, *The Kurds*.
22. *Hawar* was published between 1932–35 and 1941–43. Celadet Alî Bedir-Xan is also referred to as Celadet Alî Bedirxan, Jeladet Ali Bedir Khan, Jeladet Aali Bedr Xan, Celadet Ali Bedirkhan, Mir Jeladet and Celadet Elî Bedirxan.
23. Nebez, Jamal, 'The Kurdish Language: From Oral Tradition to Written Language', lecture published by Washington Kurdish Alliance, London (2004), pages 57, 59–61.
24. Izady, *The Kurds*. 'Yazdanism'. Reproduced by the *Encyclopaedia of Kurdistan* available at <www.kurdistanica.com>.
25. McDowall, *Modern History of the Kurds*, page 10.
26. Ibid., page 11.
27. Izady, *The Kurds*, page 135.
28. McDowall, *Modern History of the Kurds*, page 11.
29. Ibid., page 12.
30. Kurdish Partnership. Available at <www.kurdish-partnership.com/religion.html>.

2 KURDISH HISTORY

1. *The Encyclopaedia of World History: Ancient, Medieval and Modern*, 6th edn, edited by Peter N. Stearns (Boston: Houghton Mifflin, 2001). <www.bartleby.com/67/>. [19/01/2005]; McDowall, David. (2000), *A Modern History of the Kurds* (London: I.B. Tauris), page 115.
2. *Encyclopaedia of World History*; McDowall, *Modern History of the Kurds*, page 115.
3. Wilson, Woodrow, *Fourteen Points Speech* (1918). Available from <http://usinfo.state.gov/usa/infousa/facts/democrac/51.htm>.
4. Fromkin, D. (1989), *A Peace to End All Peace* (Avon Books), page 258.
5. Mosul vilayet was the area of Northern Iraq which bordered Turkey.
6. McDowall, *Modern History of the Kurds*, page 129.
7. Ideology supporting the recovery of former territory that used to belong to a country but is now under foreign rule.
8. McDowall, *Modern History of the Kurds*, page 130.
9. Ibid., page 131.
10. The Syrian border was not officially established at this stage.
11. See Appendix 1 for the text of Sèvres, Articles 62–64.
12. McDowall, *Modern History of the Kurds*, page 142.
13. Supporters of Mustafa Kemal Atatürk and, today, adherents to his Turkish nationalist ideology and *raison d'état* and protectors of the nation and state.
14. McDowall, *Modern History of the Kurds*, page 140.
15. Ibid., page 138.
16. Ibid., page 142.
17. The Treaty of Lausanne: Part III; Article 38.
18. This party was established in 1945.

19. Ghassemlou, A.R. (1993), 'Kurdistan in Iran', in Chaliand, G. (1993), *A People Without a Country: The Kurds and Kurdistan* (London: Interlink Books), pages 111–12.
20. Chaliand, *People Without a Country*, pages 211–12.
21. The 1934 Turkish Law of Resettlement divided the area into three zones. Inhabitants would be resettled from the mountainous zone for security reasons; Kurds would be resettled into the Turkish majority zone; and the final zone would see the Kurdish population diluted by settling Turks within it. This policy continued until 1946. Yildiz, Kerim and Tom Blass (2004), *The Kurds in Iraq: The Past Present and Future* (London: Pluto Press).
22. The 'Fayli' Kurds are Kurdish people who lived in Baghdad, in provincial centres such as Mandali, Khanaqin, Shahriban, Zuhayrat, Ba'quba, Kirkuk, and in surrounding areas.
23. Middle East Watch and Physicians for Human Rights (1993), *The Anfal Campaign in Iraqi Kurdistan: The Destruction of Koreme* (USA: Human Rights Watch & Physicians for Human Rights) provides a case study on the village of Koreme and the events of the Anfal campaign.
24. U.S. Department of State Bureau of Public Affairs (14 March 2003), *Saddam's Chemical Weapons Campaign: Halabja: March 16, 1988*. Available from <www.state.gov/r/pa/ei/rls/18714.htm>.
25. See also Faleh 'Abd al-Jabbar, 'Why the Intifada Failed', in Hazelton, Fran (ed.) (1994), *Iraq since the Gulf War: Prospects for Democracy* (London: Zed Books), chapter 7.

INTRODUCTION TO PART TWO

1. Meaning 'Appeal' in Kurdish.
2. McDowall, David (2000), *A Modern History of the Kurds* (London: I.B. Tauris), page 467.
3. Ibid.
4. Ismet Cherif Vanly, in Kreyenbroek, P.G. and S. Sperl (1992), *The Kurds: A Contemporary Overview* (Oxford: Routledge), page 148.
5. McDowall, *Modern History of the Kurds*, page 466.

3 SYRIAN HISTORY: 1918–2005

1. McDowall, David (1998), *The Kurds of Syria* (London: KHRP), page 6.
2. Ibid.
3. Hendriques, John (ed.) (2003), *Syria: Issues and Historical Background* (New York: Nova Science Publishers), page 73.
4. Ibid.
5. Particularly the al-Yousef and Shamdin families of Hayy al-Akrad in Damascus. McDowall, David (2000), *A Modern History of the Kurds* (London: I.B. Tauris), pages 467–8.
6. Hinnebusch, Raymond (1990), *Authoritarian Power and State Formation in Ba'thist Syria: Army, Party and Peasant* (Oxford: Westview Press), pages 71–2.

7. Ibid., page 72.
8. For example, in 1949, under Colonel Husni Za'im and in November 1951 under Adib al-Shishakli. Tachau (1994), *Political Parties of the Middle East* (London: Mansell), pages 504–5.
9. Hinnebusch, *Authoritarian Power and State Formation in Ba'thist Syria*, page 83.
10. Kaplan, Robert R. (February 1993), *The Atlantic Online*, 'Syria: Identity Crisis'. Available from <www.theatlantic.com/issues/93feb/kaplan. htm>.
11. The Syrian Communist Party was also largely considered to be a Kurdish political party. Its ranks were drawn mainly from among Kurds, who were attracted to the promotion of equality, freeing of the oppressed masses, etc. Its former leader, Khalid Bakdash (deceased) was Kurdish. Many Kurds left the SCP in the 1950s due to a conflict of ideology between Kurdish nationalists and communists. The early Kurdish parties were greatly influenced by its ideology and many continue to be.
12. McDowall, *The Kurds of Syria*, pages 16–17.
13. The Kurdish Democratic Party of Syria 1963.
14. Mullah Mustafa Barzani was the leader of the Barzan confederation of Kurdish tribes in northern Iraq and leader of the Kurdistan Democratic Party of Iraq. After his death in 1979 his position was taken over by his son, Mas'ud Barzani.
15. Seale, Patrick (1988), *Asad: The Struggle for the Middle East* (California: University of California Press), page 67.
16. Human Rights Association of Syria (November 2003), *The Effect of Denial of Nationality on Syrian Kurds* (Damascus: HRAS). Available from <www. hras-sy.org>.
17. See Human Rights Association of Syria, *Effect of Denial of Nationality on Syrian Kurds*; Human Rights Watch (October 1996), *Syria: The Silenced Kurds* (HRW); Tharwa Project (9 August 2004), *Special Report: The Plight of the Denaturalized Kurds*, 'Al Hassakeh "foreigners": Eternal suffering, nightmare of lost identity'. Available from <www.tharwaproject.com/ English/Main-Sec/Files/Kurds/Hasakah.htm>.
18. McDowall, *The Kurds of Syria*, pages 25–6. See also Tharwa Project, (9 August 2004), *Special Report: The Plight of the Denaturalized Kurds*, 'Kurdish Bidouin in Syria'. Available from <www.tharwaproject.com/English/Main-Sec/Files/Kurds/Syrian%20Bidoun.htm>.
19. George, Alan (2003), *Syria: Neither Bread nor Freedom* (London: Zed Books), page 6.
20. The 'Alawi is the religious sect to which Hafiz al-Asad and his son, Bashar al-Asad belong. The 'Alawi inhabit the mountainous and coastal regions in the west of Syria. The primary towns of this region are Lataqiyya and Tartus.
21. Perthes, Volker (1995), *The Political Economy of Syria Under Asad* (London: I.B. Tauris), pages 36–7; Zisser, Eyal (2001), *Asad's Legacy: Syria in Transition* (London: Hurst & Co), page 7.
22. Zisser, *Asad's Legacy*, page 7.
23. Perthes, *Political Economy of Syria Under Asad*, page 37.

24. Officially, in the Constitution, this is called the 'Corrective Movement'. Van Dam, Nikolaus (1996), *The Struggle for Power in Syria* (London: I.B. Tauris), page 68.
25. Winckler, Onn (1999), *Demographic Developments and Population Policies in Ba'thist Syria* (Brighton: Sussex Academic Press), page 124.
26. Human Rights Watch, *Syria: The Silenced Kurds*, page 13.
27. Ibid.
28. Ismet Cherif Vanly, in Kreyenbroek, P.G. and S. Sperl (1992), *The Kurds: A Contemporary Overview* (Oxford: Routledge), page 162.
29. Ibid.
30. McDowall, *The Kurds of Syria*, page 28.
31. Winckler, *Demographic Developments and Population Policies in Ba'thist Syria*, page 124.
32. Ibid., pages 126–7.
33. Ibid.
34. See for example, Heydemann, S. (1999), *Authoritarianism in Syria: Institutions and Social Conflict 1946–1970* (USA: Cornell University Press); Hinnebusch, *Authoritarian Power and State Formation in Ba'thist Syria*; Perthes, *Political Economy of Syria Under Asad*.
35. Seale, *Asad: The Struggle for the Middle East*, page 169.
36. Ibid.
37. Perthes, *Political Economy of Syria Under Asad*, page 4.
38. For further information on the intended succession of Basil al-Asad, see Zisser, Eyal, 'Syria: The Renewed Struggle for Power', in Ma'oz, Moshe (ed.) (1999), *Modern Syria: From Ottoman Rule to Pivotal Role in the Middle East* (Brighton: Sussex Academic Press), pages 39–40.
39. International Crisis Group (11 February 2004), *Syria Under Bashar (II): Domestic Policy Challenges*. Available from <www.icg.org/home/index. cfm?id=2516&l=1> at page 5.
40. Ibid., at page 6.
41. Ibid.
42. Ibid.
43. Al-Asad, Bashar, Inaugural speech. Available from <http://moi-syria. com>.
44. Human Rights Watch (2002), *World Report*, page 2.
45. For a detailed account of the Damascus Spring see George, *Syria: Neither Bread nor Freedom*.
46. Two outspoken independent MPs, Riyadh Sayf (arrested 6 September 2001 for 'violating the constitution') and Mamoun al-Homsi (arrested 9 August 2001 for 'insulting the constitution', 'opposing the government' and informing foreign elements) who held such forums are now in prison. Amnesty International (2 March 2003), *Syria: elections opportunity to release independent MP* (AI Index: MDE 24/010/2003); Human Rights Watch (2002), *World Report*.
47. Petitions included The Statement of 99, The Statement of 1000, and 'Towards a National Social Contract in Syria'. For text see George, *Syria: Neither Bread nor Freedom*, pages 178–93.
48. Kader, Alan (2001), *The Kurdish Cause in Western Kurdistan* (London: WKA), page 26.

49. In the year 2001. See Human Rights Watch, *World Report* (2002 and 2003) for examples. On 23 December 2002 journalist Ibrahim Hamidi, who has also written on the Kurds of Syria, was detained on charges of publishing false information. MEIB (January 2003), *Intelligence Briefs: Syria*, 'Arrest of Hamidi Sparks Outrage Abroad', (vol. 5, no. 1). Available from <www.meib.org/articles/0301_sd.htm>. Also, two outspoken Kurdish politicians from the Kurdish Yeketi Party were arrested on 12 December 2002 following their demonstration outside parliament.
50. Human Rights Association of Syria (April 2004), *The Qamishli Incidents and their Consequences in Syrian Cities* (Damascus: HRAS), available from <www.hras-sy.org>; Amnesty International (16 March 2004), *Syria: Mass arrests/Fear of torture and ill-treatment* (AI Index: MDE 24/019/2004 and MDE 24/020/2004); Amnesty International (6 April 2004), *Syria: Amnesty International calls on Syria to end repressive measures against Kurds and to set up an independent judicial enquiry into the recent clashes* (AI Index: MDE 24/029/2004).
51. Human Rights Association of Syria (March 2004), 'The Qamishli Incidents and their Consequences in Syrian Cities' (press release). Available from <www.hras-sy.org>.
52. Human Rights Watch (19 March 2004), *Syria: Address Grievances Underlying Kurdish Unrest*. Available from <http://hrw.org/english/docs/2004/03/19/syria8132.htm>.
53. See Part Three of this book.

4 SYRIAN STATE STRUCTURE

1. Al-Asad characterized his coup as a Corrective Movement within the revolution which would merely restore it to the party line. Hinnebusch, Raymond (2002), *Syria: Revolution From Above* (Oxford: Routledge), page 65.
2. Syrian Human Rights Committee (18 February 1999), *The Massacre of Hama (1982) ... Law application requires accountability*. Available from <www.shrc.org.uk/data/aspx/d1/1121.aspx>.
3. George, Alan (2003), *Syria: Neither Bread nor Freedom* (London: Zed Books), page 16.
4. Syrian Human Rights Committee, *Massacre of Hama*.
5. Human Rights Association of Syria (April 2004), *The Qamishli Incidents and their Consequences in Syrian Cities* (Damascus: HRAS). Available from <www.hras-sy.org>.
6. Perthes, Volker (1995), *The Political Economy of Syria Under Asad* (London: I.B. Tauris), page 154.
7. Article 16 of the Syrian Constitution.
8. Perthes, *Political Economy of Syria Under Asad*, page 157.
9. Ibid., page 156.
10. Ibid., page 154.
11. Ibid., page 156.
12. Article 84 of the Syrian Constitution.

13. International Crisis Group (11 February 2004), *Syria Under Bashar (II): Domestic Policy Challenges*. Available from <www.icg.org/home/index.cfm?id=2516&l=1> at page 4.
14. Articles 95 and 109 of the Syrian Constitution.
15. Articles 107 and 114 of the Syrian Constitution.
16. Articles 93 and 94 of the Syrian Constitution.
17. Articles 98 and 99 of the Syrian Constitution. Although having provided reasons, if the Assembly again approves them by a two thirds majority, the President of the Republic has to issue them.
18. Article 111. The President also assumes legislative authority between individual sessions of each people's Assembly, although any legislation issued during these periods must be referred to the first session of the People's Assembly.
19. Articles 101 and 103 of the Syrian Constitution.
20. Articles 111 and 113 of the Syrian Constitution.
21. Articles 115 and 117 of the Syrian Constitution.
22. Articles 115 and 127 of the Syrian Constitution.
23. The Parliament is represented by the 'President of the Assembly' or Prime Minister.
24. Articles 50 and 51 of the Syrian Constitution.
25. Article 63 of the Constitution.
26. Perthes, *Political Economy of Syria Under Asad*, page 166.
27. Article 71 of the Constitution.
28. Perthes, *Political Economy of Syria Under Asad*, page 164. George, *Syria: Neither Bread nor Freedom*, page 87.
29. United Nations Human Rights Committee (25 August 2000), *Second Periodic Report of States Parties due in 1984: Syrian Arab Republic* (CCPR/C/SYR/2000/2), pages 70–1.
30. Perthes, *Political Economy of Syria Under Asad*, page 166.
31. In the referendum of 10 July 2000, the Ba'th Party won 135 of 167 seats that went to PNF parties. The remaining 83 seats went to independent candidates. In the presidential elections of March 2003, the Ba'th Party won 167 of the total 250 seats, leaving the real proportion of Ba'th to non-Ba'th parliamentarians the same.
32. Perthes, *Political Economy of Syria Under Asad*, page 168.
33. George, *Syria: Neither Bread nor Freedom*, page 74.
34. Perthes, *Political Economy of Syria Under Asad*, pages 170–1.
35. Lesch, David W., 'History and Political Culture: Obstacles to Integration', in Ma'oz, Moshe (ed.) (1999), *Modern Syria: From Ottoman Rule to Pivotal Role in the Middle East* (Brighton: Sussex Academic Press), pages 63–4.
36. Most major enterprises were nationalized by the government in the 1960s during the height of socialist ideology and economic policies adopted at the same time were intended to address existing regional and class disparities. Many of these policies still exist today, hampering the country's economic growth. Despite reforms in the 1990s, the Syrian economy is still affected by low levels of investment, relatively low industrial and agricultural productivity and poorly performing public sector companies. US Department of State (August 2004), *Background Note: Syria*. Available from <www.state.gov/r/pa/ei/bgn/3580.htm>.

37. World Bank (September 2004), *Country Brief: Syria*; World Bank (August 2004), *Syrian Arab Republic Data Profile for 2003*, taken from World Development Indicators Database. Both available from <www.worldbank. org/>.
38. US Department of State, *Background Note: Syria*.
39. World Bank, *Country Brief: Syria*; World Bank, *Syrian Arab Republic Data Profile for 2003*.
40. US Department of State, *Background Note: Syria*.
41. Ibid.
42. Ibid.
43. Ibid.
44. Ibid.
45. World Bank, *Syrian Arab Republic Data Profile for 2003*.
46. US Library of Congress, *Country Studies: Syria, 1987*, 'The Judiciary'. Available from <http://lcweb2.loc.gov/frd/cs/sytoc.html>.
47. Preamble of the Syrian Constitution, 1973.
48. Article 1(3) of the Syrian Constitution.
49. Article 1(1) of the Syrian Constitution.
50. Articles 38 and 37 respectively of the Syrian Constitution.
51. Legislative Decree no.51(5) of 22 December 1962.
52. See Article 19 (1998), *Walls of Silence* (London), page 21; Syrian Human Rights Committee (20 February 2001), *Special Report – Repressive Laws in Syria*, available from <www.shrc.org.uk/data/aspx/d4/254.aspx>.
53. Middle East Watch/Human Rights Watch (1991), *Syria Unmasked* (HRW), page 24.
54. Article 19, *Walls of Silence*, page 21.
55. Syrian Human Rights Committee, *Special Report – Repressive Laws in Syria*.
56. See for example Amnesty International (20 October 2004), *Syria: Further information on: Fear of torture and ill-treatment / unlawful detention / incommunicado detention – Arwad Muhammad 'Izzat Al-Buchi (m), aged 45, engineer* (AI Index: MDE 24/072/2004); Amnesty International (28 September 2004), *Syria/Australia: Torture and ill-treatment / medical concern / incommunicado detention, Ayman Ardeli* (AI Index: MDE 24/064/2004); Amnesty International (21 September 2004), *Syria: Fear of torture / incommunicado detention, 'Abd al-Salam Assaqqa* (AI Index: MDE 24/068/2004); Amnesty International (26 April 2004), *Syria: Prisoners of conscience / fear of torture* (AI Index: MDE 24/038/2004).
57. Amnesty International (19 January 2005), *Syria: Torture and ill-treatment / possible unfair trial* (AI Index: MDE 24/003/2005); Syrian Human Rights Committee (18 February 2005), *Military Prosecution brings 18 Kurdish Detainees Before Court*, available from <www.shrc.org.uk/data/aspx/d2/2062.aspx>.
58. Article 131 of the Syrian Constitution.
59. Article 132 of the Syrian Constitution.
60. Article 136 of the Syrian Constitution.
61. Article 139 of the Syrian Constitution.
62. Article 145 of the Syrian Constitution.
63. Article 147 of the Syrian Constitution.

64. Articles 131 and 133 of the Syrian Constitution.
65. Middle East Watch/Human Rights Watch, *Syria Unmasked*, page 85.
66. Ibid.
67. Article 19, *Walls of Silence*, pages 20–1.
68. United Nations Human Rights Committee (25 August 2000), *Second Periodic Report of States Parties due in 1984: Syrian Arab Republic* (CCPR/C/SYR/2000/2), page 81 at para. 360.
69. Perthes, *Political Economy of Syria Under Asad*, page 222.
70. Ibid.

5 REGIONAL RELATIONS

1. Laizer, Sheri (1996), *Martyrs, Traitors and Patriots: Kurdistan after the Gulf War* (London: Zed Books), page 107.
2. Although Israel has never expressed a desire for confrontation with the Kurds, and defined Turkey's Kurdish problem as being an internal affair which needed no bilateral cooperation agreement.
3. Daoudy, Marwa, 'Water, Institutions and Development in Syria: A Downstream Perspective from the Euphrates and Tigris', for the World Commission on Dams. Available from <www.dams.org/kbase/submissions/showsub.php?rec=env108>.
4. See for example Kurdish Human Rights Project (August 2003), *Newsline* Issue 23 (London: KHRP).
5. Over 450,000 Kurdish refugees arrived in Turkey and on the Turkish border with Iraq, while an estimated 1,400,000 Kurds entered Iran. According to the UN High Commissioner for Refugees, the rate of influx was unprecedented in the 40-year history of the UNHCR. Cook, Helena (1995), *The Safe Haven in Northern Iraq* (London: University of Essex Human Rights Centre & KHRP), pages 37–8.
6. Ibid., page 36.
7. Ibid., page 37.
8. Farouk-Sluglett, Marion, and Peter Sluglett (2001), *Iraq since 1958: From Revolution to Dictatorship* (London: I.B. Tauris), page 299.
9. Yildiz, Kerim and Tom Blass (2004), *The Kurds in Iraq: The Past Present and Future* (London: Pluto Press), pages 71–2.
10. Republic of Turkey Ministry of Foreign Affairs (13 February 2005), *Press Release No.23 Regarding the Results of the Iraqi Elections* (unofficial translation). Available from <www.mfa.gov.tr/MFA/HomePageBottomPart/NO23_13February2005.htm>.

6 WATER RESOURCES AND CONFLICT

1. Quotes taken from 'World Commission on Dams, Dams and Development: a new framework for decision making', Earthscan, London, 2000, page 251; Curtin, F., 'Transboundary Impacts of Dams: Conflict Prevention Strategies', Working Paper prepared for World Commission on Dams (WCD), in Millington, P., 'River Basin management: Its role in Major Water

Infrastructure Projects', WCD Thematic Review, prepared as an input to the World Commission on Dams, Cape Town, 2000, page 113.

2. Materials and notes under this heading are taken from KHRP (July 2002), *Downstream Impacts of Turkish Dam Construction on Syria and Iraq* (London: KHRP), pages 13–14.

3. Materials and footnotes under this heading are taken from KHRP, *Downstream Impacts of Turkish Dam Construction on Syria and Iraq*, pages 13–14.

4. Dolatyar, M. and T.S. Gray (2000), *Water Politics in the Middle East: A Context for Conflict or Co-Operation?* (Basingstoke: Macmillan Press), page 121.

5. Cited in Philip Williams and Associates (PWA) (July 2001), *A Review of the Hydrological and Geomorphic Impacts of the Proposed Ilisu Dam*, Report for The Corner House, San Francisco.

6. Materials and footnotes under this heading are taken from KHRP, *Downstream Impacts of Turkish Dam Construction on Syria and Iraq*, page 13.

7. Allan, J.A. (2000), *The Middle East Water Question: Hydropolitics and the Global Economy* (London: I.B. Taurus), page 72.

8. Plans for the Ilisu Dam in Turkey, along with other dams which subsequently became part of the GAP project were first mooted in the 1950s. The same period saw Russian engineers conducting hydro development studies on the Syria reach of the Euphrates. See Allan, *Middle East Water Question*, page 72; Ilisu Dam Campaign and others, *If the River Were a Pen: The Ilisu Dam, the World Commission on Dams and Export Credit Reform* (Oxford: The Ilisu Dam Campaign), page 9; Altinbilek, D., 'The Ilisu Dam Project', in Turkish Embassy (2000), *Water and Development in Southeastern Anatolia: Essays on the Ilisu Dam and GAP* (London), page 31.

9. Petrella, R., *The Water Manifesto: Arguments for a World Water Contract* (London: Zed Books), page 45. The Tabqa High Dam was completed in 1973.

10. Allan, *Middle East Water Question*, page 73.

11. Interview with Mr Waleed Mu'allim, Deputy Minister for Foreign Affairs, 31 January 2002.

12. Materials and footnotes under this heading are taken from KHRP, *Downstream Impacts of Turkish Dam Construction on Syria and Iraq*, pages 15–17.

13. Marsh, N., 'Water Wars', UK Defence Forum, page 6.

14. In 1977, the Turkish government's State Hydraulics Works department (DSI) drew together all its planned programmes for the Euphrates and Tigris basins under one package – subsequently named the GAP project. In 1989, the Turkish government established the Southeastern Anatolia Project Regional Development Administration (GAPRDA) to oversee the GAP project and to ensure coordination between the agencies and institutions concerned. The GAP Higher Board is the most senior decision-making body of GAPRDA and is responsible for decisions pertaining to planning, design and work programmes. The Board is headed by the Minister of State in charge of GAP, the Minister of State responsible for

the State Planning Organization and the Minister for Public Works and Reconstruction.

15. According to the GAP administration, just over 50 per cent of this figure will be spent on dams and irrigation infrastructure. As of February 2000 – 30 years after the project was first launched – the Turkish government had raised just 43.3 per cent of the total projected expenditure. See Unver, Olcay, 'The Southeastern Anatolia Project (GAP): An Overview', in Turkish Embassy, *Water and Development in Southeastern Anatolia*, pages 14–15.

16. Sahan, E., S. Mason, A. Gilli, and A. Zogg (2000), 'Southeastern Anatolia Project in Turkey – GAP', Swiss Federal Institute of Technology, Zurich, page 1.

17. Interview with Syrian officials. These figures include all the projects planned on tributaries of the Tigris and Euphrates. The more generally cited figure of 22 dams and 19 power plants only covers major components of the GAP project.

18. The figure of 27 billion kilowatt hours of electricity takes no account of abstraction of water for irrigation. Once this is taken into account, the figure would be reduced. See Unver, 'Southeastern Anatolia Project (GAP): An Overview', pages 15–16.

19. Southeastern Anatolia Regional Development Administration <www.gap.gov.tr>. Cited in Sahan et al., 'Southeastern Anatolia Project in Turkey – GAP'.

20. Altinbilek, 'The Ilisu Dam Project', page 30.

21. Unver, 'Southeastern Anatolia Project (GAP): An Overview', page 19.

22. Ibid., page 16.

23. According to the GAP administration, 'a little over $2 billion has come from international institutions and the equivalent of $1.5 billion is coming from a build, operate and transfer scheme on the Euphrates River from a European consortium'.

24. Materials and footnotes under this heading are taken from KHRP, *Downstream Impacts of Turkish Dam Construction on Syria and Iraq*, pages 19–22.

25. Materials and footnotes under this heading are taken from KHRP, *Downstream Impacts of Turkish Dam Construction on Syria and Iraq*.

26. Unver, 'Southeastern Anatolia Project (GAP): An Overview', page 16.

27. Information supplied by Syrian officials, who also supplied the following more specific figures: existing irrigated area, 26,312 ha; area under development, 97,744; area where implementation has still to be scheduled, 447,768.

28. Government of Iraq (2002), *Position Paper Indicating Iraq's Position on the Utilization of the Tigris River Waters* (Baghdad). Syrian officials put the figure at 8 Bm^3, since they take account of evaporation from reservoirs.

29. Ibid.

30. Information supplied by Syrian officials. Onal Ozish of the Ninth of September University, Turkey, gave a figure in 1993 of 16.2 Bm^3; Ihsan Bagis of Hacettepe University (1989) put the figure at 16.7 Bm^3.

31. Government of Iraq, *Position Paper Indicating Iraq's Position on the Utilization of the Tigris River Waters*.

32. In 2000, the weekly *Sout Al Talaba* (*Students' Voice*) quoted Iraq's Irrigation Minister Mohamoud Diyab Al Ahmad as stating: 'The construction of dams and projects on the Euphrates and Tigris has caused Iraq sustained damage ... and led to great shortages in waters coming to Iraq.' 'Such huge Turkish projects place Iraq in a difficult situation.' See 'Iraq urges Turkey to reach water-sharing plan', Reuters, 16 April 2000.
33. Government of Iraq, *Position Paper Indicating Iraq's Position on the Utilization of the Tigris River Waters*.
34. Dolatyar and Gray, *Water Politics in the Middle East*, page 144.
35. This figure is derived from a Syrian analysis of GAP documents. It covers land already brought into irrigation through GAP (149,440 ha); land where work is underway to install irrigation (130,191 ha); and an area (811,572 ha) reported in the GAP general plan but where implementation has still to be scheduled. Information supplied by Syrian officials.
36. Information supplied by Syrian officials. The 9 Bm^3 figure is for irrigation water only. The higher figure – 16.9 Bm^3 – also takes into account evaporation and water losses from GAP reservoirs and is thus a more realistic estimate.
37. Information supplied by Syrian officials.
38. Materials and footnotes under this heading are taken from KHRP, *Downstream Impacts of Turkish Dam Construction on Syria and Iraq*.
39. Information supplied by Syrian officials.
40. Kolars, J. and W.A. Mitchell (1991), *The Euphrates River and the Southeast Anatolia Development Project* (Carbondale: Southern Illinois University Press), cited in Daoudy, M., 'The Development of the Euphrates and Tigris Basins: An Assessment of Upstream Development (Turkey) on Downstream Riparians (Syria)', Submission to the World Commission on Dams, Presented at the Africa/Middle-East Regional Consultation, December 1999, available from <www.dams.org>.
41. Government of Iraq, *Position Paper Indicating Iraq's Position on the Utilization of the Tigris River Waters*.
42. Information supplied by Syrian officials.
43. Materials and footnotes under this heading are taken from KHRP, *Downstream Impacts of Turkish Dam Construction on Syria and Iraq*.
44. Quoted in Dolatyar and Gray, *Water Politics in the Middle East*, page 148.
45. 'Sharing Mesopotamia', *The Economist*, 13 November 1999, page 81.
46. 'Syria, Turkey and the water tension', *Asharq Al-Awsat*, 13 February 2001.
47. Turkey had originally announced that the flow would be blocked for 16 days, but relented after protests from Syria and Iraq. See Turkish Embassy, *Water and Development in Southeastern Anatolia*, pages 68–9.
48. Allan, *Middle East Water Question*, page 73.
49. Turkish Ministry of Foreign Affairs, quoted in Allan, *Middle East Water Question*, page 73.
50. For a Turkish view, see 'Water Disputes in the Euphrates-Tigris Basin', <www.mfa.gov.tr/grupa/ad/adg/adgb/Chaplc.HTM>. The paper states: 'Before the impounding period, Turkey released more water than the commitment of 500 m^3/s which is undertaken by Turkey in accordance

with the provisions of a Protocol signed in 1987 with Syria. Turkey has thus created an opportunity for the downstream countries to accumulate this additional water in their own reservoirs. In this context, 768 m³/s of flow has been released at the Turkey–Syria border within the period starting on 23rd November 1989 and ending at the beginning of the impoundment process on 13 January 1990. Water coming from the tributaries which join the Euphrates between the Ataturk Dam and the Turkish–Syrian border has also continued to flow into Syria in the slice of time between 13 January and 12 February 1990, covering the impounding period. Thus, the total amount of water crossing the border between 23 November 1989 and 12 February 1990 has amounted to 3.6 Bm³, corresponding to an average value of 509 m³/s. Therefore, even in this period of 82 days – which also covers the one month impounding period – Syria has received more water than the committed quantity of 500 m³/s … Water in the Ataturk Dam has reached the level of 15 Bm³ during the January 1990–September 1991 period. In the same period, 27 Bm³ of water has been released to the downstream riparian countries on the basis of the 500 m³/s. As these figures indicate, Turkey could have long before concluded the filling of the dam, if it had completely cut water flow to its southern neighbours. Not opting for such a course of action is a proof of Turkey's good intentions and of its sensitivity not to cause damage to its neighbours.'
51. Ibid.
52. Measurements put the annual average at 487.67 m³/s. See Ministry of Irrigation in Syria (1999), 'Average monthly discharge (m³/sec) of the Euphrates river at Jarablus – Syria' (Damascus).
53. Dolatyar and Gray, *Water Politics in the Middle East*, page 145.
54. It is estimated by UNICEF that economic sanctions against Iraq contributed to the deaths of some 500,000 Iraqi children a year. For the period 1990 to 2000, UNICEF found that of 188 countries surveyed, Iraq suffered the worst change in mortality levels amongst children under five years old. Child mortality rates in Iraq actually more than doubled during the decade. The resigning UN Assistant Secretary General and Humanitarian Coordinator in Iraq told the UK newspaper the *Independent* in 1998, 'We are in the process of destroying an entire society. It is as simple and terrifying as that. It is illegal and immoral.' For further details of the impacts of sanctions, see <www.notinournames.org>. For details of the UNICEF report, see <www.unicef.org/newswire/99pr29.htm>.
55. Lists of equipment that was held up in this process were supplied by Iraqi sources and included water pressure filters, pumps, pipes and hoses.
56. Materials and footnotes under this heading are taken from KHRP, *Downstream Impacts of Turkish Dam Construction on Syria and Iraq*, pages 22–3.
57. For technical details of the dams, see DSI website: <www.dsi.gov.tr>.
58. The Iraqi Embassy in Ankara gave a note to the Turkish Ministry of Foreign Affairs on 17 March 1993. Syria similarly handed a note to the Turkish Embassy in Damascus on 18th July 1993. See 'Water Disputes in the Euphrates-Tigris Basin'.

59. De Villiers, M. (1999), *Water Wars: Is the World's Water Running Out?* (London: Weidenfeld and Nicolson), page 255.

60. In July 2000, the Syrian Minister of State for Foreign Affairs stated in a letter to Friends of the Earth (England and Northern Ireland) that, 'The Government of the Republic of Turkey has not officially informed, consulted, or negotiated with us about the implementation of the Ilisu Dam Project on the Tigris, as stipulated by the rules of international law and the relevant agreement on the Tigris river and other agreements concluded between the two countries.' Iraq has similarly stated that 'construction of the dam will constitute a breach of international law and it would seriously harm Iraq's rights to the river waters'. In August 2000, Dr Fahmy Al-Qaysi, Director of the Legal Department of Iraq's Ministry of Foreign Affairs, stated, 'The State of Iraq did not receive any official notification from the State of Turkey concerning its plans to construct the Ilisu Dam, and learned about the Turkish side's intentions through media reports.' See Letter to Friends of the Earth from Nasser Kaddour, Syrian Minister of State for Foreign Affairs, 3 July 2000; L.N. Al-Saidi, Iraqi Interests Section, Embassy of the Hashemite Kingdom of Jordan, Letter to Friends of the Earth, 24 March 1999; Dr Fahmy Al-Qaysi, Director of Legal Department, Ministry of Foreign Affairs, Letter to Friends of the Earth, 18 August 2000.

61. Turan, I., 'International Aspects of Water Issues', in Turkish Embassy, *Water and Development in Southeastern Anatolia.*

62. Philip Williams and Associates (PWA), *A Review of the Hydrological and Geomorphic Impacts of the Proposed Ilisu Dam.*

63. Materials and footnotes under this heading are taken from KHRP, *Downstream Impacts of Turkish Dam Construction on Syria and Iraq,* page 25.

64. As Mustapha Dolatyar and Tim Gray note: 'Syria and Iraq took every opportunity offered by diplomacy to prevent upstream developments or at least to modify them.' If Turkey is now adopting a more conciliatory position, argue Dolatyar and Gray, this is largely due to Syria and Iraq's diplomatic conduct. See Dolatyar and Gray, *Water Politics in the Middle East,* page 146.

65. Turkey has insisted that any agreement on the Tigris and Euphrates must also include an agreement on use of the Orontes (Asi) River, which flows through territory disputed by Syria and Turkey. Syria refers to the territory as Iskenderun, whilst Turkey calls it Hatay province. As Mustapha Dolatyar and Tim Gray note in their study of water politics in the region: 'If a general water agreement were to cover the Orontes, both the Syrians and the Turks think it would imply recognition of Hatay as Turkish.' See Dolatyar and Gray, *Water Politics in the Middle East,* page 149.

66. Interview with Mr Waleed Mu'allim, Deputy Minister for Foreign Affairs, 31 January 2002.

67. Interview with Mr Waleed Mu'allim.

68. Ministry of Foreign Affairs and Ministry of Irrigation, 'The Division of Waters in International Law: Facts on the Joint Waters with Turkey', Baghdad, Iraq, 1999.

69. On 4 September 2000, for example, the League passed the following resolution (6017) expressing concern over potential UK funding for the proposed Ilisu Dam on the Tigris: 'The League's Council, seeking to participate in finding a just solution to the issue of the use of the waters of the Euphrates and Tigris rivers, issued resolution number 5965 dated 28.3.00 expressing its concern regarding Turkey's continual building of dams and other projects on the Euphrates and Tigris rivers without prior consultation with the two other riparian states in which the rivers' courses also run, particularly in view of the serious damage which these projects would cause both qualitatively and quantitatively to these waters, including pollution of the waters flowing into Syria and Iraq, and the serious effects this would have on drinking and irrigation waters, and the damage done to the environment. It expressed its concern in connection with the British Government's intention to positively consider giving credit guarantees to finance the "Ilisu" Dam project on the river Tigris, and called upon the British Government to respond to the protests of official and unofficial bodies, both Arab and non-Arab, regarding the finance of this project.'

70. Materials and footnotes under this heading are taken from KHRP, *Downstream Impacts of Turkish Dam Construction on Syria and Iraq*, pages 37, 44.

71. *The Ilisu Dam: A Human Rights Disaster in the Making*, KHRP, November 1999 (reporting on the implications of the Ilisu Hydro-Electric Power Project, Batman Province, Southeast Turkey, following a fact-finding mission to the region); *If the River were a Pen*, published by KHRP, 2000 (report of a fact-finding mission to the Ilisu Dam region in October 2000, undertaken by KHRP, the Ilisu Dam Campaign, The Corner House and other parties); *The Ilisu Dam: Displacement of Communities and Destruction of Culture*, KHRP, October 2002 (review of the Ilisu Dam project and report of fact-finding mission to the Ilisu Dam region in June 2001); *Downstream Impacts of Turkish Dam Construction on Syria and Iraq*, KHRP, July 2002 (report of fact-finding mission to Syria and Iraq in July 2002). All available from KHRP.

7 INTERNATIONAL RELATIONS

1. Quote from George W. Bush, current president of the USA in his State of the Union Speech of 2 February 2005.

2. Libya has held observer status since 1999.

3. European Union, *Syria: Country Strategy Paper 2002–2006 & National Indicative Programme 2002–2004*. Available at <http://europa.eu.int/comm/external_relations/syria/csp/index.htm>. The most recent NIP for 2005–06 states that economic reform is beginning to take place, but slow economic growth and rapid population and workforce growth cause further pressure on the authorities to increase the pace of these reforms. The NIP states that Syria must stimulate growth and employment, diversify the economic structure and reduce reliance on oil revenues, undertake comprehensive reforms to improve the business environment,

rationalize and improve the quality of the public sector, strengthen the rule of law, and promote and modernize the health and education system.

4. European Union (19 October 2004), IP/04/1246. Available from <http://europa.eu.int/comm/external_relations/syria/intro/ip04_1246.htm>.
5. European Union (10 December 2003), IP/03/1704. Available from <http://europa.eu.int/comm/external_relations/syria/intro/ip03_1704.htm>.
6. European Union (19 October 2004), IP/04/1246.
7. European Union (Council), *Foreign Policy: fight against the proliferation of weapons of mass destruction*. Available from <http://ue.eu.int/cms3_fo/index.htm>.
8. European Union (Council) (3 December 2004), Progress Report on the Implementation of Chapter III of the EU Strategy Against the Proliferation of Weapons of Mass Destruction (15246/04/ PESC 1040/CODUN 41/ CONOP 59).
9. See for example (8 August 2002), *Declaration by the Presidency on behalf of the EU on human rights in Syria*. Available from <www.europa-web.de/europa/03euinf/01GASP/syria.htm>.
10. European Union (Council) (13 October 2003), *Annual Report on Human Rights*, Section 4.4.5: The Middle East.
11. European Union Committee on Foreign Affairs, Human Rights, Common Security and Defence Policy (13 April 2004), *Annual Report on Human Rights in the World in 2003 and the European Union's Policy on the Matter* (PE 329.350/DEF).
12. The National Democratic Alliance is a coalition of various Syrian opposition groups.
13. Riad Al Turk's case was also covered at a hearing of the European Parliament Human Rights Working Group on 4 June 2002 (OJ C 261 E, 30.10.2003, p. 595).
14. European Union (Parliament) (13 June 2002), *Resolution on the Situation with regard to Democratic Rights in Syria, and the case of Riad Turk in particular* (P5_TA(2002)0330).
15. US Department of State (August 2004), *Background Note: Syria*. Available from <www.state.gov/r/pa/ei/bgn/3580.htm>.
16. *Syria Linked to Capture of Saddam's Half-Brother* (Reuters, 27 February 2005 06:20 PM ET).
17. *Security Council declares support for free, fair presidential election in Lebanon; calls for withdrawal of foreign forces there* (UN Press Release SC/8181 available at <www.un.org/News/Press/docs/2004/sc8181.doc.htm>).
18. *US Ambassador in Syria Summoned Home for Talks* (Reuters, 15 March 2005 11:56 PM ET). Accessed 16 February 2005
19. *Lebanese Vent Anger on Syria After Hariri Killing* (Reuters, 15 February 2005 12:17 Pm ET). Accessed 15 February 2005.
20. *Anti-Syrian Protests Mark Hariri's Funeral* (Reuters, 16 February 2005 05:14 AM ET). Accessed 16 February 2005
21. *Bush Calls on Syria to Pull Troops from Lebanon* (Reuters, 17 February 2005 10:26 AM ET). Accessed 17 February 2005.
22. *Protesters Back on Beirut Streets; US Offers Support* (Reuters, 1 March 2005, 08:32 AM ET).

23. *US Lauds Changes in Lebanon* (Reuters, 1 March 2005 06:49 AM ET).
24. *Russia, Germany Demand Syria Quit Lebanon* (Reuters, 3 March 2005 09:38 AM ET). Accessed 4 March 2005.
25. *Saudis Back Calls for Syrian Pullout from Lebanon* (Reuters, 3 March 2005 04:01 AM ET). Accessed 4 March 2005.
26. *Assad: Syria Troops to Pullback Gradually from Lebanon* (Reuters, 5 March 2005 12:33 PM ET). Accessed 8 March 2005.
27. *Syria, Lebanon Leaders Meet, Syrian Troops Pack up* (Reuters, 7 March 2005 06:03 AM ET). Accessed 8 March 2005.
28. *Syrians to Pull Back to Eastern Lebanon this Month* (Reuters, 7 March 2005 09:11 AM ET). Accessed 8 March 2005.
29. *US Says Syria Withdrawal Plan Not Enough* (Reuters, 5 March 2005 05:46 PM ET). Accessed 8 March 2005.

INTRODUCTION TO PART THREE

1. United Nations Committee on the Elimination of Racial Discrimination (26 October 1998), *Fifteenth Periodic Report of States Parties due in 1998: Syrian Arab Republic* (CERD/C/338/Add.1/Rev.1.), page 4 at para. 10.
2. Ibid.
3. Ibid., page 2 at para. 3.

8 THE CIVIL RIGHTS OF KURDS IN SYRIA

1. Human Rights Watch (October 1996), *Syria: The Silenced Kurds* (HRW).
2. Ibid.
3. Human Rights Association of Syria (November 2003), *The Effect of Denial of Nationality on Syrian Kurds* (Damascus: HRAS). Available from <www.hras-sy.org>.
4. McDowall, D. (1998), *The Kurds of Syria* (London: KHRP), page 53.
5. Articles 43 and 44 of the Syrian nationality acquisition law.
6. Human Rights Watch, *Syria: The Silenced Kurds*.
7. Ibid..
8. Human Rights Association of Syria, *Effect of Denial of Nationality on Syrian Kurds*; Human Rights Watch, *Syria: The Silenced Kurds*.
9. Human Rights Association of Syria, *Effect of Denial of Nationality on Syrian Kurds*, page 8.
10. Ibid.
11. United Nations Committee on the Rights of the Child (1997), *Summary Record of the 361st Meeting* (UN Doc CRC/C/SR.361).
12. Human Rights Watch, *Syria: The Silenced Kurds*.
13. Ibid.
14. Ibid.
15. Ibid.
16. Ibid.
17. Human Rights Association of Syria, *Effect of Denial of Nationality on Syrian Kurds*; Human Rights Watch, *Syria: The Silenced Kurds*.
18. Human Rights Watch, *Syria: The Silenced Kurds*.

19. Ibid.
20. Ibid.; Tharwa Project (9 August 2004), *Special Report: The Plight of the Denaturalized Kurds*, 'Al Hassakeh "foreigners": Eternal suffering, nightmare of lost identity'. Available from <www.tharwaproject.com/English/Main-Sec/Files/Kurds/Hasakah.htm>.
21. Human Rights Association of Syria, *Effect of Denial of Nationality on Syrian Kurds*, page 12.
22. Human Rights Watch, *Syria: The Silenced Kurds*.
23. Since the decrees of 15 October 1999 the *mukhtar* has not been allowed to issue these documents.
24. Human Rights Watch, *Syria: The Silenced Kurds*.
25. Ibid.
26. Human Rights Association of Syria, *Effect of Denial of Nationality on Syrian Kurds*, page 12.
27. World Bank (August 2001), *Irrigation Sector Report No.22602*. Available from <www.worldbank.org/>.
28. Ibid.
29. Human Rights Association of Syria (April 2004), *The Qamishli Incidents and their Consequences in Syrian Cities* (Damascus: HRAS). Available from <www.hras-sy.org>, page 9.
30. McDowall, *Kurds of Syria*, page 53.

9 THE POLITICAL RIGHTS OF KURDS IN SYRIA

1. These parties are: *Partîya Çep Kurdî li Sûriye* / *Hizb al-Yasari al-Kurdi fi Suriya* (Head: Muhammad Mousa); *Partîya Çep Kurdî li Sûriye* / *Hizb al-Yasari al-Kurdi fi Suriya* (Head: Khair al-Din Maurad); *Partî Dêmokratî Kurd li Sûriye (al-Partî)* / *Hizb al-Dimuqrati al-Kurdi fi Suriya (al-Parti)* (Head: Nusr al-Din Ibrihim); *Partî Dêmokratî Kurd li Sûriye* / *Hizb al-Dimuqrati al-Kurdi fi Suriya* (Head: Muhammad Nazir Mustafa); *Partî Dêmokratî Kurdî Sûrî* / *Hizb al-Dimuqrati al-Kurdi al-Suriy* (Head: Jamal Mullah Mahmoud); *Partîya Dêmokrata Pê verû Kurd li Sûriye* / *Hizb al-Dimuqrati al-Taqadumi fi Suriya* (Head: Abd al-Hamid Haj Darwish); *Partîya Dêmokrata Pê verû Kurd li Sûriye* / *Hizb al-Dimuqrati al-Taqadumi fi Suriya* (Head: Aziz Da'ud); *Partîya Hevgirtina Gelê Kurd li Sûrîye* / *Hizb al-Itihad al-Sha'bi al-Kurd ifi Suriya* (Head: Salah Bedr al-Din); *Partîya Welatparêz Dêmokrat ya Kurd li Sûriye* / *Hizb al-Watani al-Dimuqrati al-Kurdi fi Suriya* (Head: Tahir Sa'doun or Sifuk); *Partîya Yekîtî ya Dêmokrat Kurd li Sûriye* / *Hizb al-Wahida al-Dimuqrati al-Kurdi fi Suriya* (Head: Isma'il 'Amo); *Partîya Yekîtî ya Dimoqrati* / *Hizb al-Wahida al Dimuqrati fi Suriya* (The name of this party and its leader changes frequently); *Partîya Yekîtî ya Kurd li Sûriye* / *Hizb al-Wahida al-Kurdi fi Suriya* (Head: changes every three years).
2. Perthes, Volker (1995), *The Political Economy of Syria Under Asad* (London: I.B. Tauris), page 167.
3. Although the political parties also carry out much of the publication and distribution of Kurdish literature within Syria, Syrian laws providing for state censorship of printed material combined with the illegal nature

of the political parties reduces their efficiency in this respect and the majority of publications are produced outside Syria.

4. Article 39 of the Constitution.
5. Chaliand, Gerard (1994), *The Kurdish Tragedy* (London: Zed Books), page 87.
6. Amnesty International (29 June 2004), *Syria: Unfair trial of Kurdish prisoners of conscience and torture of children is totally unacceptable* (AI Index: MDE 24/048/2004).
7. Estimates of numbers vary considerably.
8. Human Rights Association of Syria (April 2004), *The Qamishli Incidents and their Consequences in Syrian Cities* (Damascus: HRAS). Available from <www.hras-sy.org>.
9. Ibid.
10. Syrian Human Rights Committee (17 February 2005), *Military Prosecution brings 18 Kurdish Detainees Before Court* (press release).
11. Syrian Human Rights Committee (18 February 2005), *Military Prosecution brings 18 Kurdish Detainees Before Court*. Available from <www.shrc.org.uk/data/aspx/d2/2062.aspx>.
12. Amnesty International, *Syria: Unfair trial of Kurdish prisoners of conscience and torture of children is totally unacceptable*; Human Rights Association of Syria, *Qamishli Incidents and their Consequences in Syrian Cities*.
13. Amnesty International (4 September 2003), *Syria: Fear of torture or ill-treatment / possible prisoner of conscience / legal concern* (AI Index: MDE 24/032/2003).
14. Kurdish Media.com, 30 August 2003.
15. Amnesty International (11 November 2003), *Syria: Incommunicado detention / fear of torture and ill-treatment* (AI Index: MDE 24/042/2003). Amnesty International (17 February 2004), *Syria: Further information on incommunicado detention / fear of torture and ill-treatment* (AI Index: MDE 24/013/2004).
16. Including Amnesty International and Kurdish PEN.
17. Syrian Human Rights Committee (20 February 2001), *Special Report – Repressive Laws in Syria*. Available from <www.shrc.org.uk/data/aspx/d4/254.aspx>.
18. Syrian Human Rights Committee (2004), *Annual Report*, pages 31–2. Articles 27 and 28 of Decree 50 also require media workers to be members of the Journalists Union.
19. Syrian Human Rights Committee, *Annual Report*, pages 31–2.
20. Ibid.
21. Human Rights Watch (31 January 2002), *Memorandum to the Syrian Government: Decree No. 50/2001: Human Rights Concerns*. Available from <http://hrw.org/backgrounder/mena/syria/>.
22. Ibid., at page 7.
23. Ibid., at page 5.
24. Ibid., at page 2.
25. Ibid.
26. Human Rights Association of Syria (November 2003), *The Effect of Denial of Nationality on Syrian Kurds* (Damascus: HRAS). Available from <www.hras-sy.org>, page 15.

27. Syrian Human Rights Committee, *Annual Report*, page 33.
28. Ibid.
29. Reporters sans Frontières (11 October 2004), *Three years in prison for Kurdish journalism student who posted photos on website*. Available from <www.rsf.org/article.php3?id_article=11574>; Amnesty International (17 June 2004), *Syria: Amnesty International repeats its call for the release of five prisoners of conscience held for their peaceful use of the Internet* (AI Index: MDE 24/045/2004).
30. Amnesty International, *Syria: Amnesty International repeats its call for the release of five prisoners of conscience*.
31. Syrian Human Rights Committee (2004), Annual Report, page 32.
32. Reporters sans Frontières (29 March 2004), *Government blocks access to two Kurdish websites*. Available from <www.rsf.org/article.php3?id_article=9678>.
33. Human Rights Watch, *The Internet in the Mideast and North Africa: Free Expression and Censorship: Syria*. Available from <http://hrw.org/advocacy/internet/mena/syria.htm>.

10 KURDISH CULTURAL RIGHTS

1. Human Rights Association of Syria (November 2003), *The Effect of Denial of Nationality on Syrian Kurds* (Damascus: HRAS). Available from <www.hras-sy.org>; Human Rights Watch (October 1996), *Syria: The Silenced Kurds* (HRW).
2. McDowall, D. (1998), *The Kurds of Syria* (London: KHRP), page 47.
3. For example, Circular 7014/H issued in October 1996 aimed to enforce controls on the use of languages other than Arabic in public and in the workplace.
4. Human Rights Watch, *Syria: The Silenced Kurds*.
5. Ibid.
6. Ibid.
7. Ibid.
8. McDowall, *Kurds of Syria*, pages 50–1.
9. Ibid.
10. Ismet Chefir Vanly in Kreyenbroek, P.G. and S. Sperl (1992), *The Kurds: A Contemporary Overview* (Oxford: Routledge), page 163.
11. Human Rights Watch, *Syria: The Silenced Kurds*.
12. McDowall, *Kurds of Syria*, page 17.
13. Van Dam, Nikolaus (1996), *The Struggle for Power in Syria* (London: I.B. Tauris), page 172.
14. Nikitine, Basile (1956), *Les Kurdes: Etude Sociologique et Historique* (Paris).

CONCLUSION

1. For example Zor Ava.

Bibliography

BOOKS AND ARTICLES

Chaliand, Gerard (1993). *A People Without a Country: The Kurds and Kurdistan.* London: Interlink Books

Chaliand, Gerard (1994). *The Kurdish Tragedy.* London: Zed Books

Farouk-Sluglett, Marion, and Peter Sluglett (2001). *Iraq since 1958: From Revolution to Dictatorship.* London: I.B. Tauris

Fromkin, D. (1989). *A Peace to End All Peace.* Avon Books

George, Alan (2003). *Syria: Neither Bread nor Freedom.* London: Zed Books

Ghassemlou, A.R. (1993). *'Kurdistan in Iran.'* In Chaliand, G. (1993). *A People Without a Country: The Kurds and Kurdistan.* London: Interlink Books

Hazelton, Fran (ed.) (1994). *Iraq since the Gulf War: Prospects for Democracy.* London: Zed Books

Hendriques, John (ed.) (2003). *Syria: Issues and Historical Background.* New York: Nova Science Publishers

Heydemann, S. (1999). *Authoritarianism in Syria. Institutions and Social Conflict 1946–1970.* USA: Cornell University Press

Hinnebusch, Raymond (1990). *Authoritarian Power and State Formation in Ba'thist Syria: Army, Party and Peasant.* Oxford: Westview Press

Hinnebusch, Raymond (2002). *Syria: Revolution From Above.* Oxford: Routledge

Izady, Prof. M.R., 'Kurdish History and Culture' taken from a lecture given at Harvard University (10 March 1983)

Izady, Mehrdad, 'Exploring Kurdish Origins' lecture published in *Kurdish Life* No.5, Summer (1983)

Izady, Mehrdad (1992). *The Kurds: A Concise Handbook.* USA: Taylor & Francis Inc.

Kader, Alan (2001). *The Kurdish Cause in Western Kurdistan.* London: WKA

Kreyenbroek, P.G. and S. Sperl (1992). *The Kurds: A Contemporary Overview.* Oxford: Routledge

Laizer, Sheri (1996). *Martyrs, Traitors and Patriots: Kurdistan after the Gulf War.* London: Zed Books

Ma'oz, Moshe (ed.) (1999). *Modern Syria: From Ottoman Rule to Pivotal Role in the Middle East.* Brighton: Sussex Academic Press

McDowall, David. (1996). *A Modern History of the Kurds.* London: I.B.Tauris

McDowall, David. (2000). *A Modern History of the Kurds.* London: I.B.Tauris

Middle East Watch/Human Rights Watch (1991), *Syria Unmasked* (HRW)

Middle East Watch and Physicians for Human Rights (1993). *The Anfal Campaign in Iraqi Kurdistan: The Destruction of Koreme.* USA: Human Rights Watch & Physicians for Human Rights

Nebez, Jamal, 'The Kurdish Language: from Oral Tradition to Written Language' lecture published by Washington Kurdish Alliance, London (2004)

Nezan, Kendal, 'A Brief Survey of the History of the Kurds', presented to the International Paris Conference 'The Kurds: Human Rights and Cultural

Identity' (14–18 October 1989), available in *Collated Contributions & Messages* published by Institut Kurde de Paris (March 1992)

Nikitine, Basile (1956). *Les Kurdes: Etude Sociologique et Historique*. Paris: Impr. Nationale

Perthes, Volker (1995). *The Political Economy of Syria Under Asad*. London: I.B. Tauris

Seale, Patrick (1988). *Asad: The Struggle for the Middle East*. California: University of California Press

Tachau (1994). *Political Parties of the Middle East*. London: Mansell

Van Dam, Nikolaus (1996). *The Struggle for Power in Syria*. London: I.B. Tauris

Winckler, Onn (1999). *Demographic Developments and Population Policies in Ba'thist Syria*. Brighton: Sussex Academic Press

Yildiz, Kerim and Tom Blass (2004), *The Kurds in Iraq: The Past Present and Future*. London: Pluto Press

Zisser, Eyal (2001). *Asad's Legacy: Syria in Transition*. London: Hurst & Co.

REPORTS, PRESS RELEASES AND ONLINE MATERIAL

al-Asad, Bashar, *Inaugural speech*. Available from <http://moi-syria.com>

Amnesty International (2 March 2003), *Syria: elections opportunity to release independent MP* (AI Index: MDE 24/010/2003)

Amnesty International (4 September 2003), *Syria: Fear of torture or ill-treatment / possible prisoner of conscience / legal concern* (AI Index: MDE 24/032/2003)

Amnesty International (11 November 2003), Syria: Incommunicado detention / fear of torture and ill-treatment (AI Index: MDE 24/042/2003)

Amnesty International (17 February 2004), Syria: Further information on incommunicado detention / fear of torture and ill-treatment (AI Index: MDE 24/013/2004)

Amnesty International (16 March 2004), *Syria: Mass arrests / Fear of torture and ill-treatment* (AI Index: MDE 24/019/2004 and MDE 24/020/2004)

Amnesty International (6 April 2004), *Syria: Amnesty International calls on Syria to end repressive measures against Kurds and to set up an independent judicial enquiry into the recent clashes* (AI Index: MDE 24/029/2004)

Amnesty International (26 April 2004), *Syria: Prisoners of conscience / fear of torture* (AI Index: MDE 24/038/2004)

Amnesty International (17 June 2004), *Syria: Amnesty International repeats its call for the release of five prisoners of conscience held for their peaceful use of the Internet* (AI Index: MDE 24/045/2004)

Amnesty International (29 June 2004), *Syria: Unfair trial of Kurdish prisoners of conscience and torture of children is totally unacceptable* (AI Index: MDE 24/048/2004)

Amnesty International (21 September 2004), *Syria: Fear of torture / Incommunicado detention, 'Abd al-Salam Assaqqa* (AI Index: MDE 24/068/2004)

Amnesty International (28 September 2004), *Syria/Australia: Torture and ill-treatment / medical concern / Incommunicado detention, Ayman Ardeli* (AI Index: MDE 24/064/2004)

Amnesty International (20 October 2004), *Syria: Further information on: Fear of torture and ill-treatment / unlawful detention / incommunicado detention – Arwad Muhammad 'Izzat Al-Buchi (m), aged 45, engineer* (AI Index: MDE 24/072/2004)

Amnesty International (19 January 2005), *Syria: Torture and ill-treatment / possible unfair trial* (AI Index: MDE 24/003/2005)

Article 19 (1998), *Walls of Silence* (London)

Cook, Helena (1995), *The Safe Haven in Northern Iraq* (London: University of Essex Human Rights Centre & KHRP)

Daoudy, Marwa, *Water, Institutions and Development in Syria: A Downstream Perspective from the Euphrates and Tigris*, for the World Commission on Dams. Available from <www.dams.org/kbase/submissions/showsub. php?rec=env108>

Encyclopaedia Britannica. Available at <www.britannica.com>

Encyclopaedia of Kurdistan. Available at <www.kurdistanica.com>

Encyclopaedia of World History: Ancient, Medieval and Modern, 6th edn, edited by Peter N. Stearns. Boston: Houghton Mifflin, 2001. <www.bartleby. com/67/>. [19/01/2005]

European Union, *Syria: Country Strategy Paper 2002–2006 & National Indicative Programme 2002–2004*. Available at <http://europa.eu.int/comm/external_ relations/syria/csp/index.htm>

European Union (10 December 2003), *IP/03/1704*. Available from <http:// europa.eu.int/comm/external_relations/syria/intro/ip03_1704.htm>

European Union (19 October 2004), *IP/04/1246*. Available from <http://europa. eu.int/comm/external_relations/syria/intro/ip04_1246.htm>

European Union Committee on Foreign Affairs, Human Rights, Common Security and Defence Policy (13 April 2004), *Annual Report on Human Rights in the World in 2003 and the European Union's Policy on the Matter* (PE 329.350/DEF)

European Union (Council), *Foreign Policy: fight against the proliferation of weapons of mass destruction*. Available from <http://ue.eu.int/cms3_fo/ index.htm>

European Union (Council) (13 October 2003), *Annual Report on Human Rights*

European Union (Council) (3 December 2004), *Progress Report on the Implementation of Chapter III of the EU Strategy Against the Proliferation of Weapons of Mass Destruction* (15246/04/ PESC 1040/CODUN 41/ CONOP 59)

European Union (Parliament) (13 June 2002), *Resolution on the Situation with regard to Democratic Rights in Syria, and the case of Riad Turk in particular* (P5_TA(2002)0330)

Human Rights Association of Syria (November 2003), *The Effect of Denial of Nationality on Syrian Kurds* (Damascus: HRAS). Available from <www. hras-sy.org>

Human Rights Association of Syria (2003) *Annual Report* (Damascus: HRAS). Available from <www.hras-sy.org>

Human Rights Association of Syria (April 2004), *The Qamishli Incidents and their Consequences in Syrian Cities* (Damascus: HRAS). Available from <www. hras-sy.org>

Human Rights Watch (October 1996), *Syria: The Silenced Kurds* (HRW)
Human Rights Watch (31 January 2002), *Memorandum to the Syrian Government: Decree No. 50/2001: Human Rights Concerns*. Available from <http://hrw. org/backgrounder/mena/syria/>
Human Rights Watch (2002), *World Report*
Human Rights Watch (2003), *World Report*
Human Rights Watch (19 March 2004), *Syria: Address Grievances Underlying Kurdish Unrest*. Available from <http://hrw.org/english/docs/2004/03/19/ syria8132.htm>
Human Rights Watch, *The Internet in the Mideast and North Africa: Free Expression and Censorship: Syria*. Available from <http://hrw.org/advocacy/internet/ mena/syria.htm>
International Crisis Group (11 February 2004), *Syria Under Bashar (II): Domestic Policy Challenges*. Available from <www.icg.org/home/index. cfm?id=2516&l=1>
Kaplan, Robert R. (February 1993), *The Atlantic Online, 'Syria: Identity Crisis'*. Available from <www.theatlantic.com/issues/93feb/kaplan.htm>
Kurdish Human Rights Project (2001), *If the River Were a Pen: The Ilisu Dam, the World Commission on Dams and Export Credit Reform* (London: KHRP)
Kurdish Human Rights Project (2002), *Downstream Impacts of Turkish Dam Construction on Syria and Iraq* (London: KHRP)
Kurdish Human Rights Project (August 2003), *Newsline* Issue 23 (London: KHRP)
Kurdish Human Rights Project (2003), *This is the Only Valley Where I Live: The Impact of the Munzur Dam* (London: KHRP)
Kurdish Partnership. Available at <www.kurdish-partnership.com/religion. html>
McDowall, D. (1998), *The Kurds of Syria* (London: KHRP)
MEIB (January 2003), *Intelligence Briefs: Syria, 'Arrest of Hamidi Sparks Outrage Abroad'*. (vol. 5 no. 1). Available from <www.meib.org/articles/0301_ sd.htm>
Reporters sans Frontières (29 March 2004), *Government blocks access to two Kurdish websites*. Available from <www.rsf.org/article.php3?id_ article=9678>
Reporters sans Frontières (11 October 2004), *Three years in prison for Kurdish journalism student who posted photos on website*. Available from <www.rsf. org/article.php3?id_article=11574>
Republic of Turkey Ministry of Foreign Affairs (13 February 2005), *Press Release No.23 Regarding the Results of the Iraqi Elections* (unofficial translation). Available from <www.mfa.gov.tr/MFA/HomePageBottomPart/NO23_ 13February2005.htm>
Reuters news articles available from <www.reuters.com>
Syrian Human Rights Committee (18 February 1999), *The Massacre of Hama (1982) ... Law application requires accountability*. Available from <www.shrc. org.uk/data/aspx/d1/1121.aspx>
Syrian Human Rights Committee (20 February 2001), *Special Report – Repressive Laws in Syria*. Available from <www.shrc.org.uk/data/aspx/d4/254.aspx>
Syrian Human Rights Committee (2004), *Annual Report*

Syrian Human Rights Committee (18 February 2005), *Military Prosecution brings 18 Kurdish Detainees Before Court*. Available from <www.shrc.org. uk/data/aspx/d2/2062.aspx>

Tharwa Project (9 August 2004), *Special Report: The Plight of the Denaturalized Kurds, 'Kurdish Bidouin in Syria'*. Available from <www.tharwaproject.com/ English/Main-Sec/Files/Kurds/Syrian%20Bidoun.htm>

Tharwa Project (9 August 2004), *Special Report: The Plight of the Denaturalized Kurds, 'Al Hassakeh "foreigners": Eternal suffering, nightmare of lost identity'*. Available from <www.tharwaproject.com/English/Main-Sec/Files/Kurds/ Hasakah.htm>

United Nations Committee on the Elimination of Racial Discrimination (26 October 1998), *Fifteenth Periodic Report of States Parties due in 1998: Syrian Arab Republic* (CERD/C/338/Add.1/Rev.1.)

United Nations Committee on the Rights of the Child (1997), *Summary Record of the 361st Meeting* (UN Doc CRC/C/SR.361)

United Nations Human Rights Committee (25 August 2000), *Second Periodic Report of States Parties due in 1984: Syrian Arab Republic* (CCPR/C/ SYR/2000/2)

United Nations Security Council (2004), *Security Council declares support for free, fair presidential election in Lebanon; calls for withdrawal of foreign forces there* (UN Press Release SC/8181 available at <www.un.org/News/Press/ docs/2004/sc8181.doc.htm>)

US Department of State (August 2004), *Background Note: Syria*. Available from <www.state.gov/r/pa/ei/bgn/3580.htm>

US Department of State Bureau of Public Affairs (14 March 2003), *Saddam's Chemical Weapons Campaign: Halabja: March 16, 1988*. Available from <www.state.gov/r/pa/ei/rls/18714.htm>

US Library of Congress, *Country Studies: Syria*, 1987, *'The Judiciary'*. Available from <http://lcweb2.loc.gov/frd/cs/sytoc.html>

Wilson, Woodrow, *Fourteen Points Speech (1918)*. Available from <http://usinfo. state.gov/usa/infousa/facts/democrac/51.htm>

World Bank (August 2001), *Irrigation Sector Report No.22602*. Available from

World Bank (August 2004), *Syrian Arab Republic Data Profile for 2003*, taken from World Development Indicators Database. Available from

World Bank (September 2004), *Country Brief: Syria*. Available from

Yildiz, Kerim, and Deborah Russo (2000), *Azerbaijan and Armenia: An Update on Ethnic Minorities and Human Rights* (London: KHRP)

Index

Compiled by Sue Carlton